THE CHESTNUT PIPE

◆

FOLKLORE OF SHELBURNE COUNTY

◆

Marion Robertson

◆

Foreword By
Clary Croft

Copyright © 1991, Marion Robertson

All rights reserved. No part of this book covered by the copyrights hereon may be reproduced or used in any form or by any means—graphic, electronic, or mechanical—without the prior written permission of the publisher. Any request for photocopying, recording, taping, or information storage and retrieval systems of any part of this book shall be directed in writing to the Canadian Reprography Collective, 379 Adelaide Street West, Suite M1, Toronto, M5V 1S5.

Nimbus Publishing Limited
P.O. Box 9301, Station A
Halifax, N.S.
B3K 5N5

Design: Kathy Kaulbach, Halifax

Canadian Cataloguing in Publication Data

Robertson, Marion, 1910-

The chestnut pipe

Includes index.
ISBN 0-921054-97-1

1. Folklore—Nova Scotia—Shelburne (County). 2. Shelburne (N.S.: County)—Social life and customs. I. Title.
GR113.5.N6R62 1991   398'.0971625   C91-097688-0

Printed and bound in Canada by Gagné Ltée

CONTENTS

FOREWORD	v
CREDITS	ix
INTRODUCTION	xiii
SUPERNATURAL TALES	1
BURIED TREASURE	23
SUPERSTITIONS	29
SAYINGS	45
HOME REMEDIES	59
WEATHER LORE	84
BIRD LORE	94
ANIMAL LORE	101
INSECTS AND SNAKES	108
FISH AND AMPHIBIANS	111
PLANTS, TREES AND LICHENS	114
THE LORE OF CHILDREN	121
CUSTOMS AND CELEBRATIONS	146
SEA LORE	166
GLOSSARY	203
INDEX	262

FOREWORD

The study of folklore has become an exacting science, encompassing the collecting, classification, and analysis of material from our oral and material cultures.

Modern folklore scholars not only want to know what was said and done, but also why. They need to find variants of the same information to define it as folklore. Then the material is classified and cross-referenced with other related data to help determine its context. Finally, the story, song, or saying undergoes careful analysis to establish its foundations and to help speculate where it might yet be going.

The American folklorist L.J. Davidson writes, "Folklore is the study of a popular heritage of a group held together by common interests." In fact, the term "folklore" was first coined in 1846 to help define the study of "popular antiquities." So this field is constantly changing and developing new ways of study and analysis.

There is still room, however, for the fascinating collections of local lore assembled by wonderfully inquisitive people such as Marion Robertson. These local collections are valuable records of life as it once was. And interestingly enough, they tell us a great deal about ourselves today.

Marion Robertson has given us such a collection. Hers is a vital and often first-hand account of legends, superstitions, ghost tales, cures and remedies, games, folk speech, and local oral tradition. Where a folklorist frequently looks at an area from the point of view of an "outsider," Marion Robertson recounts her stories from within the community. She has provided the reader with an intimate look at the lifestyles and beliefs of the people who inhabit the southwestern shores of Nova Scotia.

Readers wishing to explore and compare additional material will be interested in the works of Lewis Poteet and his South Shore phrase books, as well as in the 1931 collection by Arthur Huff Fauset, "Folklore from Nova Scotia" (*American Folklore Society Journal*, vol. 24). Mr. Fauset did substantial collecting in Shelburne and Yarmouth counties, and he was one of the first folklorists to assemble material from the black communities in these areas.

Of course, the foremost collector of folklore in Nova Scotia was Dr. Helen Creighton. In fact, Dr. Creighton collected from some of the very same people who inhabit the pages of Marion Robertson's work. Earl Smith, of Clark's Harbour, Shelburne County, told Marion boyhood fishing tales—for Helen Creighton, he sang folk songs such as "Grandmother's Advice" and showed her how even "quite big children" would join in the singing game "Balm O'Gilead."

Both Helen Creighton and Marion Robertson collected sea stories from Reuben Smith of Blanche, Shelburne County. Mr. Smith also sang the ancient Child ballad "Lord Bateman" for Dr. Creighton. In her notes accompanying audio recordings she made of Mr.

Smith, Helen Creighton writes, "The Smiths are fine people, and have performed many kindnesses for strangers cast away on their shores." (See audio tape AR5154, Public Archives of Nova Scotia).

But for now, you have some very interesting reading in your hands. Take yourself back to the days of making soap at home, or learn how to stuff a mattress with eel grass. Chill to actual tales of piracy and murder, delight in the story of the sheep who ate the oranges, and learn the benefits of that well-known Nova Scotia cure-all Minard's Linament, and of a pumpkin seed, a remedy that "saved a doctor's bill and even helped a horse."

Marion Robertson's collection of folk speech is very enjoyable as well. We learn about the traditional Nova Scotia custom of "boodle," which is an exchange of money or rum for a vote. During the Canadian national election campaign of 1891, this was a commonly used term. And who can forget visiting the old homestead, where late at night, without the benefit of indoor plumbing, you gently placed your "husher" on your "jingler."

Enjoy and explore this collection. You will meet some old friends and remember beliefs long forgotten. You will also discover many new and exciting stories from our Nova Scotia folk heritage.

Clary Croft
Halifax, N.S.
1991

CREDITS

Although I have written the text of this book, the voices of many have shared with me their experiences, their knowledge of old beliefs and customs, home remedies, unusual words and sayings, stories, and the lore of birds and animals. As a child growing up in Barrington, I heard many old superstitions, rhymes, games, and weather lore. From an old sea captain who came to our house "to spend the evening," and from others who had fished and sailed in pinkies, I heard sea stories and sea lore. As the years passed, I began to record in notebooks the wonderful things I heard. The pages of my many notebooks have provided the material for this book.

With the passing of years, many who shared with me their old stories and bits of folklore are no longer here. My grandparents, my father and mother, Nina and Bertram Doane; aunts and uncles; Captain George Pike, who told me the story of the *Georgie Harold;* George Hopkins, who went fishing with his father in a pinkie and scooted water on her limp sails with a scoot horn; the Micmac James Michael, who knew the story of Wokun; Lev Davis, who had a Micmac keeler and knew how to shape one from a log. Miss Belle Hopkins, Miss

Winnifred Crowell, Maria Leach, Mae Mart, and Benjamin H. Doane had stories of the supernatural and other facets of folklore. Loie Doane, who grew up in Welshtown, had Welsh stories to tell that were part of her childhood.

Evelyn Richardson shared children's rhymes that she remembered from her childhood in Clarks Harbour, as well as old home remedies and local names for sea-and shorebirds she collected from a Cape Island fisherman stormstayed on Bon Portage when she and her husband kept the light. When she was writing "Wreckwood Chair," I gave her stories that I had collected from Reuben Smith of Blanche. I have used the stories, as related to me by Reuben Smith, in this book.

Many contributed bits of sealore: Forman Atkinson of Cape Island, Milton Stoddard of Woods Harbour, and Gilbert Nickerson of Shag Harbour. Earl Smith of Clarks Harbour remembered ways of fishing from his boyhood and related many old customs and beliefs.

Mrs. Gilbert Nickerson of Shag Harbour first told me of gurry soap; Mrs. Jane Madden of Baccaro, who also made gurry soap, told me of lichens and barks she used to dye wool she sheared from her sheep, which roamed the shores of Baccaro, her sheep marks cut in their ears. Wylie Perry of Ingomar and Marion (Davis) Doane of Roseway had stories of buried treasure, and Wylie Perry had stories of a witch. Mamie Perry of North East Harbour remembered old home remedies her mother used. Gertrude Swaine of Port Saxon remembered old stories and old remedies; Preston Smith of Barrington Passage remembered many old words and customs.

In the Shelburne area, in Sandy Point and in Lower Ohio, were many who knew stories, tales of the supernatural, customs and the celebration of days. The Allen sisters, Jane, Mary, Kate and Lillian; Naomi Rowse, Mrs. Lockie Crow, Miss Belle Williams, Roy Smith, Annie Ward, Louis Thomson, Edith Devine, Mrs. Claude Smith, Donald Robertson, Mabel and Clifford Robertson, John MacKay, Mrs. Annie Bruce, Rollie Gibson, Mrs. Clifford Coutanch, Fred Bower and Bertha Harris, in Lower Ohio. In her neat ninety-year old handwriting, Mrs Allison Allen of Sable River wrote pages of old cures she and her mother brewed from bark and flowers, and her memories of children's rhymes.

Turning to today, many have shared folklore and stories. Among those who have given generously are Terry Bower and Trevor Bebb. Margaret Messenger contributed words and superstitions, and a copy of the manuscript "Down Shore Tales" by William Arthur Swim, a valuable record of fishing customs, words and stories. Many others have contributed stories, words and folklore in this book: Dorothy MacKinnon, Trudy Atkinson, Mamie Harmon and Theresa Brakeley; Irving Quinlan, Lillian Fox, Aileen MacLaren, Marion Abbott, Charlotte Grovestine, Ronald Harding, Lorn Bower, Ena Wall, Arlene and Welsford Acker, John Watt, Evelyn Smith, Josie Cofin, Billy Belliveau, Mary and Perley Townsend, William Crowell, Rev. James Hicks, Mindy O'Neil, Noble Smith, Evelyn Thomas, June Morse, Dorothy Armitage, Beverley (Ryer) Huddleston, Muriel MacKay, Grace Jones, Ruby Perry, Jack Gibson, Roger Grovestine, Betty June Smith and Ann Wickens, Grant Goodick, Wayne Butler, Blanche Lamrock, Daisy (Buskirk) Doane, Irva Cunningham, Carl Atwood, Donald Glover, Betty Lou Benham, Emily Harris, Athena Colpitts, MacDonald Hervey Leach, Gerald Bower, Elgin and Betty Davis, Herbert and Bessie Harris, and Dolores (Scott) Dallaire. Marie Amirault remembered the words of "Lizzie Dies Tonight" as sung by her old grandmother when she was ninety years old and more. Alice Doleman and Sanford Doleman who first told me of the chestnut pipe he made when a boy in Lockeport. To all I give my thanks.

Others have provided information I needed, including Alex Wilson of the Nova Scotia Museum and Eric Ruff of the Yarmouth County Museum. Millie Rogers and Pat Randall helped in other ways, and for needed information and assistance I give them my thanks. I am grateful to Dr. Diane Tye of Mount Allison University for her interest and encouragement and to Dorothy Blythe of Nimbus Publishing for her valuable assistance in the publication of this book.

Books have provided information and a background for some traditional family stories related from memory: Poole's *Annals of Yarmouth and Barrington (Nova Scotia) in the Revolutionary War;* Crowell's *History of Barrington Township and Vicinity 1604-1870.* Other books provided words and expressions as spoken by Shelburne County informants: Bill McNeil's *Voice of the Pioneer*, "These Waters off (Cape) Sable Island," an interview with Dewey Nickerson; *Lockeport Lockout*, researched by Michael Lynk and written by Sue Calhoun. Margaret Messenger's fine studies in the life and history of Cape Sable Island have provided information, especially her book *An Island Town.* From the *Coast Guard* have been gathered many examples of words and expressions recorded verbatim in reports which I have acknowledged in my collection of words. The *Journal of Education,* April 1957, provided information about the petrified woman in J.S. Erskine's article "Mud Island."

Marion Robertson

INTRODUCTION

In the very old days, the land that is now Shelburne County, on the southwestern shores of Nova Scotia, was part of that great land of the Micmacs, Megumaage. Shelburne County itself was then called Kespoogwit—"where the land goes down to the sea." As years passed, the sea that brushed the shores of Kespoogwit brought the first white men—the French, the Basques, the Portuguese. The French founded the first fishing and farming communities, and built a trading post on the harbour of Port La Tour.[1]

The Micmacs shared their knowledge of the land, the rivers, and the lakes, as well as their traditional lore, with the French settlers, and later, with the New Englanders and the Scots-Irish. Micmac ways of catching fish in a weir, of spearing eels, and of healing soon became part of the settlers' skills and customs.

The settlers brought with them their own traditions—knowledge acquired and passed from father to son, from mother to daughter. They established communities through their own efforts. They built small boats for fishing and larger sailing ships to trade in ports along the New England shores and in distant seaports in the West

Indies. They soon began to hold meetings to govern their communities, to survey and mark land into holdings. Strongly religious, they observed the Sabbath, and in 1765, those in Barrington built a meeting house that stands today—the oldest non-denominational meeting house in Canada. Just as their ancestors had left their homes to seek religious freedom and new opportunities, the New Englanders and the Scots-Irish cherished the inherent right to govern and shape the future of their land.

With their strong support of the American Revolution, they continued their trade with the New England States and, sharing their hard-earned living, helped hundreds of escaped American prisoners. As well, they concealed American privateers and their prizes in their harbours.

As the war continued, their anger grew stronger than their support of the Americans' struggle for freedom. When armed ruffians—freebooters—pretending to be licensed privateersmen came into their harbours, pillaged their houses and fish sheds, and went off with their boats, the settlers of Ragged Islands protested vigorously to the State of Massachusetts Bay that if they, who had given so much to America, were to be molested by ruffians, they wished to see no more of them "without you come in another manner."[2]

When the war was over and the Americans victorious, many hundreds of those who had been loyal to the Crown began to wish for a new British homeland. On the shores of Nova Scotia at Port Roseway, formerly Port Razair, there was land available on a deep, wide harbour where settlers could cut timber, cultivate the soil, build boats, and fish. In New York in the fall of 1782, hundreds of Loyalists banded together as the

Port Roseway Associates, and in early May 1783, they arrived in Port Roseway, soon to be named Shelburne by Governor Parr. As the months passed, other Loyalists arrived from the old British colonies and, in the fall, came several regiments of British soldiers. Several hundred Freed Blacks, former slaves of rebel masters who had accepted the British proclamation of protection, were settled on the shores of nearby Birchtown Bay.

For the Port Roseway Associates and other Loyalists who sought refuge in Shelburne, there were many disappointments. Accustomed to cleared fields and city streets, they found the rocky soil and tree-covered land that stood above the shores forbidding. When they discovered they were not to receive special consideration by the provincial administration, but were to abide by the same laws and regulations as others in the province, many were disappointed. Then land grants were delayed, and those who were anxious to clear land for farms had no land to clear. For these and other reasons, many left Shelburne to find homes in nearby communities and in distant parts of Nova Scotia. Some went to the West Indies; others returned to the United States. Shelburne faded from a town of several thousand to a town of a few hundred.

In Birchtown, several hundred Freed Blacks accepted the offer of land grants in Sierra Leone, on the west coast of Africa. After years of deprivation, they left for the land of their ancestors. People in Birchtown still speak of the caves where some of the Freed Blacks had lived—deep holes dug in the hillside covered with a slanting roof of poles.

Among others who have settled in Shelburne County were deserters from regiments and warships, and families and individuals from ships wrecked along the shores.

Some came from nearby counties; others from Scotland and Ireland. In 1818, Welsh settlers were given land for farms along the west bank of the Roseway River.

The blend of many cultures has given rise to rich folklore and stories. This book should be considered a sampler of the folklore and stories that abound in Shelburne County.

For those who are interested in tracing the origin of superstitions and beliefs, customs and words, turning the pages of books such as Frazier's *Golden Bough*, Trench's *Study of Words* and *English Past and Present* will find the old, sometimes ancient origin of words and superstitions and beliefs that have come the long way from the past to the present.

ENDNOTES

1. In 1699, Joseph Robineau De Villebon, Commandant in Acadia, 1690-1700, reporting on the forts of Acadia, listed the fort at Port La Tour as built for trade with the Natives rather than as a fortification for defence. John Clarence Webster, *Acadia at the End of the Seventeenth Century*, p. 129.

2. Edmund Duval Poole, *Annals of Yarmouth and Barrington (Nova Scotia) in the Revolutionary War*, p. 47.

SUPERNATURAL TALES

The response to the supernatural is as varied as the people who express an opinion. Even those who scoff at tales of the mysterious unknown have a strange fascination with supernatural stories, and they listen and retell them as eagerly as those who believe in an "unrevealed" world. Of the privileged few who have "rubbed shoulders" with a strange "something," some have heard sounds or have seen moving lights; others have been aware of a presence, "a darker darkness in the dark." One knew her house was haunted when she heard a woman's voice wailing above the sound of the wind blowing against her house.

Some have related strange dreams or have seen apparitions that have turned them away from an approaching disaster; others, understanding the meaning of a "forerunner," have waited for its fulfillment. Some have strived to defeat witches; others, to divert the evil force that can be set in motion when an old and long-revered superstition goes unheeded.

◆ GHOSTS ◆

"What do ghosts look like? They look like the persons they once were—but are not as solid. They are there, and are not there."

Ghosts are almost always seen or heard at night, and often in isolated places, on the roadside, in cemeteries, where pirates have buried treasure, or where an untimely death has occurred.

GHOSTS BY THE ROADSIDE

In Shelburne, there are stories of a strange man on the old Morvan Road, which once ran between Shelburne and Jordan Ferry. A number of years ago, when the road was still passable to horse-drawn wagons, a group of young people from Shelburne went to Jordan Ferry, to a Sunday-school convention. On their return, their horses stopped on Morvan Hill, and they saw, standing beside the road, a strange man dressed in a long brown duster. He came to the first wagon and, leaning against the dashboard, peered up into their faces. They spoke to him, but he did not answer. He stepped back from the road, and the horses moved on. One of the men remarked, "I've travelled all the roads of Shelburne County, but never have I seen that fellow." When they reached home, one of the girls said to her sister, "Well, we've seen the man of Morvan Hill."

◆

Several years ago, four women of Lockeport were returning in their sleigh from a temperance meeting in Jordan. It was a brilliant moonlit night, and the road was glistening with snow. Near the bridge at Lydgate, their horse stopped, and they saw, coming along the road, a man wearing a long black cape and a tall pointed hat. He turned from the road and walked into an open field and vanished.

◆

One Sunday evening, a young sea captain and his mother were driving home from church at East Jordan when their horse stopped and refused to go on. The young captain sprang from the wagon to see what was wrong and saw a man walking along the road. He called out to him, "Do you want a lift?" The man did not answer but walked on a little farther and disappeared. The horse then trudged home.

◆

In the 1920s, when he was teaching school in Churchover, a young man heard many strange stories of a hill where, long ago, three pirates had been hanged. The hill stood boldly beside the road between Churchover and Gunning Cove, and the pirates' ghosts still loitered on the hill. When travelling alone, no one passed the hill at night; travelling with others, everyone hurried along, beyond the reach of the pirates.

CEMETERY GHOSTS

There is a story of a soldier buried near a cemetery gate in Shelburne who was killed in a duel in one of the town's many taverns. Sometimes he was seen standing at attention at the gate, saluting passers-by. His arm would fall off his shoulder. He would then lift his other arm, pointing his fingers upward. It, too, fell from his body. With a horrible shriek, his head twisted and danced on his shoulders and fell to the ground.

Sometimes people saw ghostly pallbearers carrying a coffin to the same cemetery. They moved in a solemn procession up to the gate of the cemetery, whereupon they faded away.

HEADLESS GHOSTS

One of the headless ghosts seen in lonely places haunted Brass Hill, roaming the fields along the road. He was said to have been a Black named Barse who gave his name to the hill, later known as Brass Hill.

In the 1840s, a boy thought he saw the headless ghost of Brass Hill when he was on his way home to Barrington Passage. At the sight of the ghost gliding over the snow, he dashed into the bushes. As the ghost came closer, he saw a man in high white spatlatches carrying a white bag of flour across his shoulders. As the man came closer, he called out, "Hello, Ben." The boy told him that he thought he was the headless ghost of Brass Hill. "Here I've lived all my life," the man told him, "and never have I seen a headless ghost."

◆

Headless ghosts are reputed to guard buried treasure in some places. One haunts John's Island in the harbour of Port La Tour. When people approach him, he disappears, and reappears only when they run from his ghostly presence. On Gray Island, where Captain Kidd's treasure is believed to have been found, there appeared before some fortune-seekers a number of headless men. Perhaps they were the same ghosts seen at Little Port La Bear rowing to an island where treasure is buried.

HOUSE GHOSTS

"I suspect there's 'something' in all houses—even quite new houses if something vital from the past has been brought into the new house. Sometimes you know 'something' is there—even if you don't hear or see it. It's just a presence you feel."

♦

In an old house in Shelburne, when the stillness in the living room was unbroken by the slightest whisper, on several occasions people heard three bumps in a storeroom upstairs. The sound always came from one corner of the room, where a baby's swinging cradle was stored. The cradle had belonged to the great-aunt of someone living in the house at that time. When the great-aunt's baby died, shortly after her husband's death, the woman went to live with relatives and the baby's cradle was stored in the attic. A careful search of the room revealed nothing that bumped, until a hand was placed on a rocking chair that stood in front of the swinging cradle. When the hand was lifted, the chair swung backward and bumped the cradle, the cradle bumped the wall, then swung forward against the chair—three bumps.

In the same house, a young couple was awakened one night by the sound of someone at their back door, turning the handle and gently pushing at the door. As the couple listened, they heard the door open and footsteps cross the kitchen and stop midway. Accompanied by their little dog, the couple crept down the hall to the living room and into the kitchen. There was no one there. They searched the room, its cupboards, a closet, and a back stairway to the attic. The back door was securely locked on the inside, the sliding bolt firmly wedged into the door-casing.

♦

In a Shelburne house that had been vacant for several years, a young woman saw an elderly tall, thick-set man with stooped shoulders standing in one of the rooms. She knew there had been no one in the house, for she had had to unlock the door to enter. She closed her eyes and said, "There is no one here." When she opened them again, the room was empty.

She asked a woman if she remembered her grandfather, who had lived there, but the woman did not recall him. She asked an elderly lady, who had lived in Shelburne as a girl, if she remembered the old man who had lived in the house. Indeed she did.

"Was he a tall man with stooped shoulders?"

"That's a very good description of him—a tall man with stooped shoulders," she answered.

◆

In Coffinscroft, a young woman and her husband lived in a house where his grandmother and uncle had lived for many years. On January 3, 1954, in their first year in the house, many of the couple's friends came to visit. In the evening, when her husband and their friends went to call on a nearby neighbour, the young woman stepped into the living room to replenish the fire in the base-burner. As she stooped to pick up a chunk of wood, a cold blast of air struck the back of her head. She turned around to see where the cold air had come from, for there was no outside door in the living room. There, standing before her, was a man she had never seen before. He was short, dressed in an old faded cotton shirt and dark pants with suspenders. He had big ears that stood out and a large nose. He was mumbling something she could not understand. She was paralysed. At last, she made a sound, and he disappeared as if he had never been there. When she told her husband, he said, "That was Sandy. He looked just like the man you saw."

When Sandy lived in the house, he had two wood piles—one at the front of the house, on the other side of the road, and one at the back. Near the time of the full moon, the couple heard someone chopping wood in the evening. When they looked out the front windows, the sound came from the back of the house; when they looked out the back windows, the sound came from the front. The husband remembered when he was a little boy how Sandy liked to cut and split wood in the moonlight.

◆

In one of the older Barrington homes, in the stillness of the night, a soft rustling sound was heard on the stairs—the sound of a long silk skirt brushing against the treads. At the head of the stairs, the sound crossed the upper hall, moved into the bedroom, and passed through the wall of the house at one corner.

In the same house, a young woman awoke one night, and in the dim darkness of the room, she was aware of a darker darkness at the foot of the bed. As the rustling of a skirt on the stairs was heard in the dark stillness of the house, the darker darkness came to the foot of the bed, as if born of the stillness of the room.

◆

In another Barrington house, built by a young sea captain, came the sound of footsteps across the attic floor. One day, when the captain's wife heard the steps, she climbed the attic stairs, lifted the trap door, and peered into the room. To her astonishment, a man she had never seen before was kneeling in front of a sea chest that her husband had saved from an old house before it was demolished. She spoke and the man vanished.

◆

In a field near Sable River stood the home of a woman who had lived there all her youth. After she married, her husband did not want to live in the house. He insisted that she sell it and that they live elsewhere. She begged him not to force her to sell her home, but he was adamant and the house was sold. Not long after they left her beloved home beside the Sable, she died in grief and longing. After her death, a family member who had bought the house was asleep in one of the upstairs bedrooms. She awoke and to her amazement, beside the open door to the closet beneath the eaves, was an old lady in a dust cap. As she watched, the old lady disappeared into the closet.

◆

In Welshtown, a little girl, a descendant of one of the Welsh families that came there in 1818, saw a woman she would never forget. The girl's mother had sent her to the root cellar for vegetables, where she saw in the dim light, a strange woman standing by one of the bins. She was wearing a dark dress, a long white apron tied about her waist, and her hair was hidden beneath a strange cap. The girl ran back upstairs to her mother, who told her it was "old Mary" and that others had seen her in the root cellar.

◆

Not all "beings" that linger in houses are as quiet as those who rustle lightly on the stairs, or as gentle as the old lady in the root cellar. Some are noisy and frightening, as were two in houses in Shelburne. In the spare room of a house on Mowat Street where she was visiting, a young woman was awakened by the ringing of a bell. As she listened, the sound became the sharp clang of a hammer on an anvil. She thought everyone in the house must be awake, so she hurried to her friend's room. But her friend was asleep and there was no such sound in her room. When she returned to the spare room, it was still invaded by the clang of metal on metal.

Then the sound ceased, and the room became quiet. The next morning a neighbour told her that others who had slept in that room had heard the same heavy clanging.

◆

Noisy ghosts inhabited an old house on the southwest corner of Water and King Streets. In the early days it was a store and tavern. More than a century ago, a woman who lived in the house told her nieces of a drunken ghost in her living room. On one occasion, she and a friend were suddenly overwhelmed by the sound of a drunken man rolling on the floor, kicking the floor boards and shouting in slurred accents. They could see nothing, but the woman never forgot the terror of her guest as the sound continued, although no one else was in the room.

◆

In Coffinscroft, in an old house that groaned and creaked as its wooden pegs strained against the force of the wind, a woman's wailing was heard crying, "W-h-o s-t-o-l-e m-y g-o-l-d-e-n a-r-m?"

GHOSTLY LIGHTS

There are many stories of strange lights hovering over water, lights that disappear and reappear. Such a light was sighted from the shores of Ingomar. When some men of the village went in a boat to investigate, the light suddenly disappeared. They searched the water but there was no boat or buoy from whence the light could have been shining.

◆

Lights known as Dunn's have been seen over Shelburne Harbour. One New Year's Day, a couple from Sandy

Point, named Dunn, visited friends who lived on Hart's Point. That night, on their way home in their boat, they quarrelled and Dunn pushed his wife overboard into the harbour. The next morning he threw himself into the harbour, from a rock near the Sandy Point lighthouse that still bears his name. In the years since, some have seen lights on the harbour dancing toward each other, twisting and twining, then disappearing into the water.

There is another version of the story: One New Year's Day, Dunn met a friend who remarked that it was a hot day for winter. Dunn replied that it was hotter in hell. That afternoon he rowed with his wife to the middle of the harbour and drowned her and then himself. Ever since, on New Year's Eve, lights have been seen dancing up the harbour and on meeting, they disappear.

◆

A strange light hovers over Lake Deception, once known as Grand Lake for its large size. As the years passed, it became known as Lake Deception for the many islands that obscure its width and length. A number of years ago, on a brow of land bordering the lake, a club house was built for the Rod and Gun Club. One night, the club's guide saw a strange light appear above the water and move across the lake toward him. As he watched, the light took on the features of a face. He called to the people in the club house to come out, and as they watched the light move towards the shore, they too saw a man's face in the ball of light. They ran, and some of them never returned to their club house on the shores of Lake Deception.

♦ *TALES OF SECOND SIGHT* ♦

There are many tales of people with "second sight," who can see an event taking place, even though they are not present. One such person who lived in Shelburne with her daughter was sometimes aware of events as they happened to her family far away. One day, as she sat in her chair in the living-room, she felt the presence of a relative who lived in Australia giving her a message which she imparted to the others in the room. Some days later, a letter was received from the relative with the same message she had received through her mysterious gift.

On another occasion, when she was visiting relatives in Allendale, she knew that a son of the family, whom his parents had tried to persuade not to go to sea, had been drowned. Weeks later, word came that the ship on which he sailed had been wrecked and all on board had lost their lives.

These stories of her grandmother were told by a woman who had herself experienced second sight at a party when someone passed her a cup to read the tea leaves. Suddenly before her eyes there was an overturned dory beside a wharf and a man drowning. The next day, the lady who had jovially passed her tea cup to be read received word that her brother had been drowned when his dory overturned near a wharf on the Jordan River.

♦

Dorcas Page was remembered by her granddaughter as having the gift of second sight. By her marriage to James Thorborn, Dorcas had six strong sons, all of whom "followed the sea" and became captains and masters of vessels sailing out of Lockeport, near their family homestead at East Jordan. One special Christmas Day all her six sons were expected home, and for her son Howard it would be a joyous festival, for his young fianceé was waiting his return. He did not sail into Lockeport the day before Christmas as expected, and his brothers jokingly teased their mother that he would be home in time for Christmas dinner. That night, Dorcas Page was awakened by a strong wind blowing about her bed. She called to her husband that the kitchen door had blown open. He assured her that it was securely bolted. Then she knew that her son was gone, for in the wind was the sound of sails slating against a mast and a voice above the wind.

In the morning the ground was white with snow that had fallen in that sudden gust of wind that Dorcas Page had felt in the darkness, and she knew it had caught her son's vessel in its talons. No wreckage came ashore, nor was the body ever found to tell the tale of her son's lost struggle with wind and sea.

◆ *FORERUNNERS* ◆

A sign that precedes death is known as a forerunner. Sometimes a strange occurrence, a sound, a light, three knocks on a door or a sudden physical weakness foretells an approaching death.

◆

A bird as a forerunner of death was long remembered by a woman on Cape Island. When she lifted the window of her son's bedroom, a little grey bird flew into his room. A few minutes later, the boy, who was playing in the yard, picked up a tamarind pit that had been thrown out with the table scraps for the hens, swallowed it, and choked to death. Then the mother remembered the little grey bird that came to tell her of her little boy's approaching death.

◆

The death of a young man flying from Gander to Summerside was foretold by a bird that came into his parents' house in Shelburne. They had great difficulty driving the bird from the house. Later, when the message came of the plane crash, they remembered that it was the hour of his passing that the bird came into their house and struggled against leaving.

◆

A young fisherman's wife knew her husband had been drowned when his photo suddenly fell from the wall. She had begged him not to go with the other fishermen when they pushed off from a wharf in Shelburne. It was stormy weather and she wanted him to remain on shore until the bad storms of winter were over. In heavy seas, he fell overboard and was drowned. When the others came ashore she learned it was the hour when his photo fell from the wall that he was drowned.

◆

At midnight, a woman in Shelburne heard her telephone ring. A few minutes later she heard it again. She got up from her bed, telephoned the operator and asked her if she had called. The operator assured her that she had not. The next morning came a message that her brother had died at the time she heard the phone ring.

◆

For a Sandy Point woman, three knocks on her back door foretold the death of a friend. When she heard the knocks, she was surprised that someone had come to her house so early in the day. She opened the door, but there was no one there and she knew what the three knocks foretold. She waited by the door and very soon a neighbour came to tell her one of her dearest friends had died.

◆

A Lockeport woman heard the faraway sound of a ship struggling in a torrent of wind. It filled her with fear for the safety of her husband and his ship. Then the sound ceased and she knew he had passed beyond the storm. Weeks later, when ships returned from the Caribbean, the sailors told of hurricanes and great storms in the southern islands. Many ships had perished, among them, the one her husband sailed in as master.

◆

In Shelburne, the sound of footsteps foretold a father's death. In the stillness of the night his son awoke and heard soft footsteps crossing the living-room floor beneath his bedroom. He crept downstairs, but there was no one to be seen. Two days later, word came that his father had died shortly after the time he had heard footsteps.

◆

A young woman in Green Harbour, walking home one foggy night, heard footsteps behind her. When she turned and peered into the darkness there was no one to be seen. Three times she heard the footsteps; each time, there was no one in sight. In her haste to reach her front door she neglected to shut the gate. Behind her the gate slammed shut. The next day a friend died in a car accident and she knew whose footsteps she had heard.

◆

During the Second World War, in the living-room of a Shelburne home, was the cherished photo of a young man in his army uniform. One evening, one of his sisters noticed a bright light shining on the photo. She called attention to it but her mother dismissed it as being the street light shining across the glass. The sister felt something had happened to her brother, and her presentiment was remembered two weeks later when word came that he had been killed.

◆

For a Shelburne storekeeper, physical weakness hovered over him like a dark shadow at the time of a friend's fatal accident.

◆ APPARITIONS ◆

When someone appears "in person," as an apparition, it is usually a sign that a death has, or will soon, be made known.

◆

The mother of a twelve-year-old girl in Jordan Falls was very sick. One day, the girl was sent to a neighbour's house to ask for help. She ran along the path to the house, opened the door and stepped inside the porch. As she waited for the inside door to be opened, her mother stood beside her. She ran back across the field to her home and was told that her mother had died.

◆

In Shelburne, a story is told of a young sailor who was on a ship ready to sail at dawn. His mother, who had recently died, came into his cabin and told him to leave the ship. He could not ask for permission to leave, so he jumped overboard and swam ashore. The ship sailed and was later lost with all on board.

◆

In Lockeport, where many ships sailed to distant seaports a century ago, there is a story of a young man who was walking in the moonlight on Louis Head Beach. In the distance, he saw a man step from the edge of the water onto the beach, and walk toward him. Then he saw that it was his friend who had sailed weeks before to the West Indies. He ran forward to greet him, but his friend walked past him, as if he was not there.

In Lockeport there was no word of the ship the young man's friend had sailed in, and it was weeks later before he heard of his friend's fate from the the captain of the vessel. On a previous voyage, his friend had met a young lady whom he had promised to marry on his return. When they entered the port where she lived, she came on board and descended the stairway to the cabins. The doors between the captain's cabin and the young man's were open, and the captain heard the young man tell her that he had married another. In a fury she denounced him for his infidelity and cursed him for the dishonour he had brought upon her and her family. Never would there be happiness in his marriage, and she predicted disaster would fall on him. Weeks later, as he stood near the bow of the ship on a quiet moonlit night, her prediction was fulfilled: a great wave washed across the bow, and when it subsided, he was no longer there.

◆

A young man who lived in Washington came to visit his mother at her home in Coffinscroft. One evening, as they sat around the fireside with a friend, one of the women remembered she needed to borrow a flashlight to leave beside her bed. The young man went to his car for one. It was a calm, moonlit night, and, as he stepped outdoors, he saw, standing beside his car, his old grandfather who had been dead for many years. The young man gripped the railing at the side of the steps. His old grandfather said, "It's alright, Manny—you'll see, everything will be alright." 'Manny' was the name his grandfather gave him. The young man turned and went back into the house and told his mother and their friend what he had seen. His mother was not at all surprised, for she too had seen apparitions, and knew from her years of living that spirits come back to places where they have once lived or died.

One year when the young man's mother was away from her home for many months, a friend cared for the house. When he did not return home, his family came looking for him, and found he had died while sitting in the big armchair beside the living-room fireplace. Many months later, following her return to her house, she was awakened one night by a strange sound. She got out of bed and stood in the doorway opening into the living room. The room was flooded with moonlight, and there, sitting in the same chair, was the man who had cared for her house.

◆ DREAMS ◆

Interpreting dreams as messages, usually warnings of danger, have been important to families whose lives are closely linked to the sea.

◆

A young man of Barrington Passage, who sailed as mate on his brother's vessel, dreamed that he should not sail on the next voyage to the West Indies. He told his brother of his dream, and the second mate took his place. Another seaman, when he heard the story of the mate's dream, decided he too would not sail on the next voyage to the West Indies. The ship left without them and was never seen again after she left the shores of Nova Scotia.

In Barrington Passage, a woman's dream prompted her to go to the shore to look for the return of her husband's vessel. Her husband's name was Nehemiah. In her dream she walked down the slope of a hill to a wet marsh and felt the wet marsh mud seep into her shoes. Then she was on the shore looking anxiously down the passage of water that separated the mainland from Cape Sable Island. There, in her dream, she saw a vessel with its flag at half-mast. A small boat was lowered and two men rowed toward the shore. As they came close into the shore she called, "Who is it?" They answered, "It's Nehemiah."

When she awoke, she walked down the slope of the hill near her house to the marsh, and felt her feet grow damp with the wet marsh mud. When she reached the shore she looked anxiously down the passage toward the open sea. There, just as in her dream, she saw a vessel anchored with its flag at half-mast. A small boat was lowered and two men rowed toward the shore. She called to them, "Who is it?" And they answered, "It's Nehemiah."

◆ PHANTOMS ◆

There are many unusual, unexplained phenomena, which reflect the sorrow felt by tragic events, such as shipwrecks.

PHANTOM BANDS

When the east wind was blowing and a storm brewing, the people of Lockeport used to hear, off in the distance, the ghostly sound of a band playing. It was the band of the brig *Emulous,* which foundered on a reef that now bears her name.

Not far from the breakers of Emulous is Ram Island, where, on a dark night in April 1831, the *Billow,* with a regiment of soldiers on board, destined for Halifax, caught her keel. At the time, her band was playing "The White Peacock Feather." In Little Harbour, when the wind blows from the reef that caught the *Billow,* some hear a band playing that same song. There was a light seen above the *Billow* the night she struck the reef. It is still sometimes seen hovering above the reef, then it drops and is gone.

PHANTOM CARS

Phantom Cars are a recent phenomenon. Two have been seen on roads leading away from Sable River—on old Route 3 from Sable to Allendale, and on the older Sable to Jordan road that, until reconstructed as part of Route 103, was a narrow dirt road connecting the two villages.

◆

A car with four passengers and a driver was headed along the road towards Allendale. As they drove along, they saw ahead a very old car. They remarked that it must be an old Ford, one of the first, with its tail light centered on the back, jerking with the motion of the car. The driver followed behind the old Ford until the road curved just before a long stretch of straight road. Then, suddenly, the car was not there. They thought it must have turned off into a side road. But there was no side road, nor any place a car could quickly cross the roadside ditch and be lost to sight among the trees.

The second story occurred one night when a couple, driving toward Jordan, saw an old car coming toward them. It was being driven on the left-hand side of the road as was the custom in the early years of automobiles. It continued on the left, the couple in their car holding as far as they could to the right. The car still came on, until within a few inches of contact, it disappeared.

♦ *WITCHES* ♦

There are some stories that tell of the supernatural power of witches.

♦

It is said that some witches dwell in chimneys and cause the stove to smoke. Years ago, in Shelburne, an old fellow known as Soeul looked after the chimney witches. He went from house to house and fired his gun up the chimney to kill them. One day when he fired his gun up a chimney it back-fired, throwing him to the floor, yelling, "That was one mighty, powerful witch."

♦

In Ingomar some years ago there lived a woman who was believed to be a witch. They called her Charlotte and one man claimed he shot her dozens of times for putting a spell on his hens and chickens. To do this, he made a drawing of her on a board and shot the drawing with bullets filled with bits of silver cut from a coin. Before shooting Charlotte, he had someone go to her house to watch her reaction. With each shot, she cried out with a pain wherever the bullet struck the drawing, and fell to the floor when the bullet 'pierced' her knee. This would break the spell she had put on his hens, and they would run around the yard clucking.

When his wife was sick and was told she would not live, he said it was one of Charlotte's spells and shot his drawing of her. Charlotte's spell was broken and his wife lived for many years.

◆ *MISCELLANEOUS* ◆

A fascinating story told by one old-timer does not seem to fall into any of the facets of the supernatural, but was nevertheless a strange experience. As a little girl, in Barrington Passage, she discovered one morning, on her way to school, that by lifting her feet as she stepped onto a ledge of rock that extended diagonally across the road, she glided from one side of the ledge to the other as if drawn by a magnet. She was astonished, but she dared not tell the other children. Every day, when she reached the ledge, she would lift her feet and glide to the other side of the road.

Years passed and she became a professor of English in an American university. At a social hour during a conference the talk turned to strange adventures. She related, for the first time, her experience of gliding across a ledge of rock. Later, one of the professors came to thank her, for he, too, had had a similar adventure when he was a boy in Ohio, and, like herself, had never told of his singular experience.

◆

Before a bridge was built across Bloody Creek, and before the creek had a name, a man walked through the woodlands to Middle Clyde. When he returned he was asked if he had a good trip. He replied, "It was a good trip until I came to that bloody creek."

The old Micmacs knew Bloody Creek as Wokun for

a knife that lay on a rock in the creek. In Micmac stories, two young men once fought on the banks of the creek. One of them slipped and fell into the creek and his knife slide from his hands to a rock beneath the water. When the Indians lifted his lifeless body from the creek they reached for his knife, but they could not touch it even with the tips of their fingers—and they went away in awe of the strange spirit that held the knife to the rock beyond the reach of their fingers.

BURIED TREASURE

Stories of buried treasure along the shores of Shelburne County continue to this day. There are hundreds of islands and uninhabited inlets where ships could anchor in the dead of night and sailors could bury their ill-gotten gains.

♦

One of the old stories of buried treasure takes place on Apple Island, off the shores of Roseway. Near nightfall, many years ago, a strange brig was seen anchored off the coast. As darkness fell, a boat was rowed from the brig to Apple Island. In the morning, the ship was gone, and some men from Roseway rowed to the island where they found holes dug in the ground and marks where a large chest had been lifted out of one of the holes and dragged across the mud and rocks to the water's edge.

♦

Near Apple Island, on Gray Island, Captain Kidd is believed to have buried his gold. On a stormy night, some men went out to the island to dig for the gold. All went well as they dug in silence until they came to an iron box. Then one of the men shouted in triumph, and the box vanished. Men who later went to look for the treasure came away with stories of seeing headless men, presumed to be the men Captain Kidd had killed—their ghostly apparitions left to guard his treasure.

◆

Undeterred by headless ghosts, a man in Carleton Village bought a mineral detector, and he and a number of men went out to the island. He prodded around with his rod until he found the site of the treasure. They began to dig and soon came upon a great chest of gold. One of the men laughed and everything disappeared, even the hole they had dug. One man who helped dig the hole declared he saw the great chest of gold and would fight anyone who told him he was "seeing things."

◆

Another Gray Island story is of a great chain fastened from a rock down into the ground to buried treasure. People who have gone to the island in recent years and have searched for the chain could find no trace of it nor the rock where it had been fastened.

◆

It is believed there is buried treasure on John's Island in Port La Tour Harbour. Some men went out to the island one dark night, taking with them a young boy to watch for anything unusual that might appear as they dug. They tied him to a stunted tree so he could not run away. They dug in silence and were well down in the treasure hole when there was a tremendous noise, like a great clap of thunder, that rolled around them. They took off for their boat, forgetting the boy, but he arrived at the boat before them, tree and all.

◆

There were once two brothers who went out to dig for buried treasure on John's Island. When they started for the island the sky was clear and the land bright with moonlight. By the time they were halfway across the harbour, the sky became overcast, and on reaching the island a thunderstorm drove them back to the mainland. This happened every time they set out to dig for buried treasure on John's Island.

◆

Many years ago, a strange ship was sighted at nightfall anchored near Cape Negro Island. The island's inhabitants thought that the men from the ship came ashore for water. The ship was gone by morning and on the shore, near where the men had landed, were holes dug deep into the earth and rough marks of a chest having been drawn to the water's edge. The residents believed that the ship's company had an old chart marking the site of buried treasure.

◆

Big Island in Cape Negro Harbour is said to be one of the islands where Captain Kidd buried his treasure, and where he killed a man and buried him with the treasure, to guard it forever. A few years ago, some men from Port Clyde rowed out to the island to dig. They got down close to the treasure when a ghost—a pirate ghost—stood before them and frightened them off the island.

◆

On the shores of Shelburne Harbour are several sites reputed to be places where pirates buried their stolen treasure. One of these is near the Tea Chest at Sandy Point. Some years ago, some men dug for treasure there, but found nothing. Then they remembered the old wive's tale that if the throat of a black cat was slit, the blood would flow toward the treasure. This they did, but still had no luck. Years later, others tried to find the treasure. They dug until they came to planks. They cut the throat of a black cat and the blood circled into a pool. One of the men spoke, and the next morning when they searched for the hole, it had disappeared, and no trace was found of the place where they had dug.

◆

On the further shore of Shelburne Harbour, near Birchtown on the western side of the bay, it has long been believed that there is buried treasure. When some very old coins were found on the shore of Shelburne Harbour, two boys from Sandy Point rowed across the bay to dig. There, they met an old man who told them what to do. First, they must cut a stick from an alder and with it mark a circle on the ground where they believed the treasure was buried. Then, at midnight, they were to step inside the circle and dig in silence. They followed the old man's instructions and dug and dug until they came to a blood-red layer of heavy sand welded into a solid mass. They chipped at it, but it was not the treasure they sought, so they walked away. But they never forgot the old man's instructions.

◆

Blue Island or Green Island, as it was sometimes known in earlier days, in Jordan Bay, off the shores of Green Harbour, is rife with old stories of buried treasure. One evening, years ago, a mysterious ship anchored near the island, and the inhabitants watched, but did not see anyone come ashore. In the morning, the mysterious ship was gone. In Brick Hill, just above where the ship had anchored, they found a deep hole, and on the shore below were marks as if a heavy chest had been dragged to the water's edge.

◆

Another Blue Island story involves a lady resident who had heard tales of Captain Kidd's treasure being buried on the island and decided to investigate. She started to dig. About three feet down, she came to yellow paint. Below the paint were many treasures buried in the clay. She told her neighbours and they looked for the hole that she had dug, but it had disappeared. But the paint was real. She painted her house yellow.

◆

Among the stories about the expulsion of the Acadians from the Cape Sable area are tales of buried treasure. When the Acadians knew the English were coming to burn their houses and drive them off their land, their priest took the altar vessels from the church, near the sand hills in Villagedale, and buried them, declaring, "No Englishman will ever find what is sacred to us." The sand hills, then at the water's edge, drifted over the land and over the Acadian cellars. When the French came back many years later, they could not find the spot where their treasures had been buried. A few years ago some men of Villagedale told their friends that they had found the altar vessels, but they did something wrong and the vessels disappeared.

◆

Buried treasure has also been the source of a few pranks. Some men once buried an iron pot on Battery Hill,[1] in Shelburne, and told an old black man that they would show him where he could dig for treasure. On a moonlit night they went with him to show him the place. One of them draped himself in a sheet and took along a chain to rattle, then he hid himself in the bushes near the buried pot. With shovels and pickaxes, the others went with the old man to the hill. It was not long before his pickaxe clanged on the iron pot, and the man in the bushes stepped into the open, rattling his chain. The old man shouted "It's gold—devil's gold!" and ran down the hill and up the street, the "ghost" running after him, jangling his chain.

◆

The only buried treasure one man in Ingomar could remember was rum. When a rumrunner put into Ingomar and caught the keel of his boat on a ledge, every fish boat for miles along the shore went to her rescue. The rum vanished, no one knew where. Years later a new culvert was installed for an improved highway. There, hidden in the old drain, were bottles and bottles of rum.

ENDNOTES

1. *King's Bounty,* p. 115. Battery Hill was bulldozed into a pond and the land levelled for the erection of the Irving Oil Company storage tanks.

SUPERSTITIONS

Superstitions from the past linger like shadows in the background of the present, for old beliefs are not lightly cast aside. For some, old superstitions grip their lives; others dismiss them with a nod and a chuckle and knock on wood for fun.

Many superstitions have been recorded elsewhere in this book, in animal, bird and insect lore, as well as in sealore. There are many other superstitions: ways to gain good luck, ways to discourage bad luck, ways to understand and interpret events and omens, and what to expect if old taboos are disregarded.

STARS AND MOON

For good luck, wish on a falling star or on the first star of the evening, saying,

Star light, star bright,
First star I've seen tonight.
Wish I may, wish I might,
Have the wish I wish this night.

Or wish on the new moon, bowing three times to the moon, saying,

New moon I'm seeing,
Wish I may, wish I might,
Have the wish I wish this night.

Wishes must never be told if they are to come true. When wishing on the new moon, the moon must first be seen over the right shoulder, never the left shoulder, for fear of bad luck. In the fall, one must wish on a full moon or hard work will follow for the next 30 days.

PENNIES AND TWO-DOLLAR BILLS

Find a penny, pick it up, and all day you will have good luck. First step on the penny, then pick it up. A penny lying head up, keep it; tails up, give it to a friend. To enhance the good luck of finding a penny, give it to the first person you meet, or put the penny in your left shoe, or throw it over your left shoulder and wish for good luck. Never pass by a penny or any coin without picking it up, or you will forever be poor. It is good luck to be given a new purse with a penny in it; without a penny you are doomed to always be poor.

It will bring bad luck your way to have a two-dollar bill in your purse. Two-dollar bills are "hoodoo" and will not be accepted by some fishermen, even as change when paying a bill. To break the bad luck of a two-dollar bill, nip a tiny corner off it. For good luck, fold a bill lengthwise when placing it in your purse and you will never be penniless.

KNIVES, FORKS, AND SPOONS

Strangers and guests who "stir with a knife, stir up strife." A knife must never be placed on a table with the blade up, and a sharp-edged knife or any sharp point, such as a needle, must never be given as a gift. Sell a sharp point for a penny and save your good luck.

Cutlery on the table has significance. An extra spoon signifies a lady guest; an extra knife, a man; an extra fork, a stranger. For a crossed knife and fork, expect a wedding. "Drop a spoon, a stranger soon," meaning a child will come your way; drop a knife, a woman guest; a fork, a man. The handle points in the direction from which he will come. To spin a butter knife is a sign of a fight.

EXPECTING GUESTS

There are other ways to know when to expect a guest and when to expect a stranger.

When tea was brewed from tea leaves, if a stem floated on the surface of a cup of tea, you could expect a guest.

Bite the stem; if soft, expect a woman; if hard, expect a man. To find out when the guest is coming, place the stem on the back of your hand and whack it with your other fist, saying with each whack, "Today, tomorrow, next day, sometime." The day of your guest's arrival will be signified by the blow which makes the stem fall off your hand.

When a broom falls across a doorway, or through an open doorway, a stranger is coming to your house.

To go in one door and out another will bring a stranger.

A dropped dish towel also signifies a stranger coming. If it falls open, it will be a woman; if in a knot, a man.

SALT

Since the years when fine-grained table salt was a luxury, to spill salt is bad luck. To overcome the bad luck, pinch a few grains of the spilt salt between your right-hand fingers and throw them over your left shoulder.

NUMBERS AND DAYS

The significant numbers are 7, for good luck, and 13, for bad luck. Over Friday the 13th hovers bad luck, except for those born on Friday the 13th, for whom it is a good luck day. Work started on Friday will never be finished; besides, to start work on Friday will bring a rainstorm. Of all the days of the week, Friday is the "fairest or the foulest."

Monday is always a good day to watch, for, "as goes Monday so goes all the week." Work hard on Monday, work hard all the days of the week; guests on Monday, guests all the week.

SHOES AND CLOTHING

Shoes can be good luck and bad luck. Old shoes thrown at someone starting a trip, such as a bride and groom, bring good luck. Shoes lying upside down on the floor are bad luck to their owner who should quickly turn their soles to the floor. Shoes must never be put on a bed or on a table, and when dressing, a woman must first put on her right shoe, a man, his left shoe. New shoes that creak are protesting vigorously that they have not been paid for.

A shirt, dress or any garment put on inside out, must not be removed and turned right side out for twelve hours. If the hem of a dress turns up, the wearer will soon have a handsome new dress. To mend a dress when it is being worn means the wearer will always be poor.

A loose thread on your clothing means a visitor is on the way, or you are going on a trip. A dropped glove must always be picked up by someone other than its owner. A hat must never be thrown on a bed for this will bring you bad luck.

COLOURS

Some colours bring bad luck, especially green. Green for a boat is a bad colour. Clothing must never be green, nor anything in a house, not even a strip of green in wallpaper or a green leaf on a cup. Some will not allow plants in the house, nor wild flowers with green leaves.

THE LIFE CYCLE

Surrounding the cycle of life—birth, childhood, marriage and death—are long remembered superstitions.

During pregnancy, an expectant mother must not reach her arms above her head or bend forward, nor crouch down, for fear of binding the umbilical cord around her baby's neck.

A mother marks her baby, it is believed, with the tips of her fingers when she craves during her pregnancy any unobtainable food, such as strawberries in winter. To prevent a visible birthmark, she should touch her back, but never her face, neck, hands or arms, where the red strawberry of her longing would mark her baby for life.

To tell the sex of an unborn baby, a threaded needle is dangled over a pregnant mother. If the needle describes a circle, the baby is a girl; if it swings back and forth, a boy; if it does not move, the baby will be stillborn.

A child born with a veil or caul will always be lucky and will never drown. A man in Sandy Point carried his caul with him when he went to sea, assured if he was tossed into treacherous waters that he would not drown.

To tickle the bottom of a baby's foot will cause the baby to stutter and stammer.

There is an old saying that a good-looking baby will grow homely, while an ugly baby will be a good-looking adult.

The seventh son of a seventh son will be psychic.

An old birthday custom to help a child slip through the next year of growth is to butter a child's nose. To the birthday spanking of one spank for each year are added two spanks—one for good luck and one to grow on. Alternatively there might be one spank for each year, "a pinch to grow an inch, and pull your hair so you won't swear."

Along with superstitions are the answers for every child's query, "Where do babies come from?" In addition to the old standbys, "brought by a stork," and "the doctor brings a baby in a black doctor's bag," there is the answer, "from under a cabbage leaf."

MARRIAGE

To fall upstairs foretells a wedding. Others say, if you tumble upstairs you won't marry this year.

Two knives at a place setting, a knife and a fork crossed on a table, and four hands crossed when shaking hands, are all signs of a wedding near at hand.

There are ways to find a perfect mate. To find your husband's age, take one half your age and add seven. To find the first letter of his or her name, take an apple and twist the stem, saying one letter of the alphabet for each twist. When the stem snaps from the apple, that will be the first letter of your beloved's name. But be cautious, "Change the name but not the letter, change for worse and not for better."

June is the best month for weddings and happy is the bride on whom the sun shines.

A bridal dress must never be made on a Friday, and should never be yellow—"ashamed of your fellow." If the dress must be sewn on a Friday, the night before, spread the cloth on the table, with the pattern, scissors and pins all ready to cut the dress.

The groom must not see his bride's gown until the wedding and must not see the bride on their wedding day before the ceremony.

For good luck and future happiness the bride must wear,

Something blue and something new,
Something old and something borrowed.

Before her engagement a young woman must never wear a ring on her wedding finger, and following her marriage she must never remove her wedding ring.

Before leaving on her honeymoon, the bride tosses her bouquet above the heads of her guests to be caught by one who will become the next bride. Bridesmaids must remember, "three times a bridesmaid, never a bride."

DEATH

There are many lingering superstitions that surround the dying, and signs that foretell death (*See also* Chapter 1).

To dream of a birth there will be a death in the family, and if a small grey bird comes into a house it is a forerunner of a death in a family. In Sandy Point, the arrival of a stray black-billed cuckoo is a dark omen for its plaintive *ku-ku-ku* from the dark depths of the evergreens signal illness and deaths in the community. Only when it leaves or is driven from the shadows where it lurks among the evergreens, will the sick recover.

Three knocks on the door foretell the death of a friend or relative, and when cattle and horses, in an open field in the night, are restless there is a death in the community.

When a picture falls from the wall, there will be a death in the family or the death of a close friend.

To drive a nail into wood on Sunday is driving a nail in your coffin, and an inch worm on your clothing is measuring you for your coffin.

Death comes in threes; hear of one, hear of three.

If someone dies on a Friday, there will be two more deaths before sunset on Sunday. Keeping a body over a weekend signals that someone close to the deceased will die within a few days.

An open winter, one with no snow, an open graveyard.

If it rains in a open grave, there will be three more deaths, or someone will die within the coming week.

In the past, a palm branch on a door-casing was a symbol of a death within the house, and most funerals were held in the home of the deceased. Christmas decorations hung on a door are a forewarning of death.

It is bad luck to meet and pass a funeral procession, and if you watch a hearse go out of sight, one of your friends will die.

In an old belief, to dream of the dead is to hear from the living.

THE HUMAN BODY

In old superstitions itching has significance. If your left hand itches you will get some money; if your right hand itches, you will shake hands with a stranger. When your feet itch, you are going on a journey; if it is the bottom of your feet, you will walk on strange land. If your left ear burns, someone is saying bad things about you; if your right ear burns, someone is saying something good. If your ears ring, you will hear of a death. A right eye that itches means a woman visitor is on her way to see you; the left eye, a man. When your nose itches you are going to be kissed.

Red hair marks a quick temper.

A left-handed child forced to write with the right hand will stutter.

White spots on fingernails mean the following: count each finger from your thumb, saying, "friends, foes, lovers, beaux, travels to go." The number of spots on each nail tells how many friends, foes, lovers, beaux, and travels to go will come your way.

A child's tooth must never be thrown away for fear a cat will find it and the tooth that grows to replace the old one will be a cat's tooth. For good luck, put your tooth under your bed pillow and a fairy will come in the night and exchange the tooth for a coin.

An amputated arm must be buried carefully, for if the fingers are not straight, the patient will suffer pain in a phantom arm.

When someone sneezes, say, "God bless you," to frighten away the devils.

ROCKING CHAIRS AND THREE LAMPS BURNING

To rock an empty rocking chair will bring unhappiness into a house, even death. Never leave a chair rocking after sitting in it, for bad luck will follow you. To see a chair rocking in an empty house foretells disaster. Turn away quickly and never enter the house again.

In the days of sailing ships, there was an old saying, "Three lamps aburning and nary a ship at sea." It was condemnation of a spendthrift, one who burned three lamps, but had no means to pay for the oil. In more modern days to have three lamps burning on a table is bad luck, if nothing more serious than three cracked lamp chimneys.

CHRISTIAN DOORS AND WAYS TO CONFUSE EVIL SPIRITS

Six-panel doors, known as Christian doors, keep out the devils and witches that lurk around houses. "The devil he can fuss and fume, but he can't pass a Christian door." A Christian door, placed near a wall inside a house, if opened wide against the wall will confine any devils and witches in the corner and free the room from evil spirits.

Say "break a leg" to confuse the evil spirits, or better still, knock on wood to deafen whatever evil spirits are in the wood or in a room, or touch the wood of a cross.

HORSESHOES

Horseshoes are another way to discourage evil spirits from entering a house or a barn. They must be nailed to the lintel above the door, with the two tails upward, the toe downward. Horses and cattle can pass beneath the horseshoe, evil spirits cannot. To find and keep horseshoes is also good luck.

"DON'T"

There are many old superstitions buttressed with "don't."

Don't pass anyone on the stairs. Turn back and wait until there is no one on them.

Don't step over a broom handle.

Don't sweep after dark, or you will sweep away your wealth.

Don't throw away dirt swept from the floor, for to throw away swept dirt is to throw away your luck.

Don't pass food "against the sun." Pass food from East to West.

Don't cut your toenails before going to bed or you will be plagued with nightmares.

Don't cut your fingernails on Friday or Sunday.

Don't brush your hair after dark for fear of bad luck.

Don't open an umbrella in a house. To do so will bring unhappiness.

Don't bring a four-leaf clover into a house.

Don't let anything come between you and a friend when walking down the street together.

Don't rock an empty rocking chair or the wind will blow.

Don't kill a spider. Bad luck will come your way if you do.

Don't kill a swallow, or the cows will give bloody milk.

Don't walk under a ladder.

Don't step on a crack in the sidewalk. "Step on a crack, break your mother's back."

Don't watch anyone as they go out of sight. Either it will bring bad luck to the person being watched, or you will never see that person again.

Don't be the first person to speak when you walk into a silent room.

Don't shake the crumbs from a tablecloth after dark.

GOOD LUCK SUPERSTITIONS

For good luck, wish on a load of hay.

The first time you eat in a house, make a wish for good luck.

It is good luck to carry a horseshoe in your pocket, and more good luck to nail a horseshoe above a door, the toe of the shoe downward, to prevent your good luck from sliding through the open end of the shoe.

To find a four-leaf clover brings good luck.

It is good luck to cross your fingers when you are scared.

It is especially good luck to shake hands with a chimney sweep.

It is good luck to be given a purse with a penny in it, for then you will never be poor.

The good luck in finding a penny is doubled when you give it to the first person you meet.

Carrying the right front paw of a rabbit in your pocket brings good luck.

To pick up a pin is good luck, but turn the sharp point away from you before picking it up.

Find a button, pick it up; two holes good luck, four holes exceeding good luck.

Spoon the bubbles from a freshly poured cup of tea, keeping the bubbles well away from the edge of the cup; sip them from the edge of the spoon and money will come your way.

When things are going wrong, sit on a handkerchief and change your bad luck to good luck.

BAD LUCK SUPERSTITIONS

It will bring bad luck to a hunter if a woman or a girl steps in front of him when he is preparing to go hunting. A little girl who grew up in Welshtown in the 1890s was told by her friend when she went to her house to play, not to step in front of her father when he was getting his gear ready to go hunting, for he would hit her hard if she did.

To stick a needle in a spool of thread is an invitation to bad luck.

It is bad luck to go in one door and out another. It will bring bad luck your way if you turn a loaf upside down in the pan while the bread is being baked in the oven.

To spin a butter knife is bad luck for it will bring on a fight.

If you sing before breakfast, you will cry before nightfall.

It is bad luck for a black cat to cross your path. Turn around and walk the other way.

It will bring bad luck to go skating at the full moon.

For a flag, or a flag pole, to fall is very bad luck. There is an old story in Shelburne that the flag fell to the ground as Governor Parr named the town Shelburne, and those who saw it fall knew their town would never become the great and prosperous city they had envisioned.

It is bad luck to start a journey and then turn back for something forgotten. To avert the bad luck that will come your way, sit down and count to one hundred, or throw some salt over your left shoulder.

It is bad luck to turn the hands of a clock backward, counter-clockwise, for it will take time off your life.

It will bring bad luck to a family to build a house on an old foundation.

It is bad luck to hand anyone a sharp object. Place it on a table or a chair to be picked up.

Break a mirror, seven years bad luck.

MISCELLANEOUS

Someone is thinking about you when you mention their name in place of a name you intended to say.

If you say something slightly questionable and want to make your statement come true say, "Cross my heart and hope to die."

If you say something and want it to come true, knock on wood.

If you say something at the same time as someone else, you must clinch each other's little finger and make a wish. To make your wish come true pull the fingers hard; whoever's finger is first released gets the wish.

A stolen plant grows best. When given a plant, never say thank you, or else the plant will not grow.

If you clean and wash windows on a fine day, it will rain on the morrow.

When a lot of baby carriages are out on the road before it is spring, or even in the early spring, there will be a bad winter the next year.

If a picture or a mirror falls from the wall, you will hear bad news, probably the death of a friend.

If you wipe your hands on the same towel with another person you will, one day, have a fight with that person.

It is very unlucky to predict or to pretend to know the future. When bidding a friend goodbye say, "I'll see you again, God willing," for only God knows the future, and to say, "I'll see you again," displeases God.

SAYINGS

Many old sayings go deep into the past, and express a meaning far beyond the words spoken. In their homespun wisdom, few sayings remain unique within a set boundary, and few of these well-known sayings in Shelburne County are unknown elsewhere, for, "a good thing goes a long way."

Bon auger days; pot (pod) auger days: the good old days.

Three generations from coat sleeves (coat tails): a family that has fallen from affluence to poverty.

From shirt sleeves to shirt sleeves in three generations: the rise and fall and rise of a family's fortune.

I wasn't born in the woods to be scat by an owl: a hefty response to a threat.

Gone like Spencer's eels: In Allendale a man named Spencer had a boat load of eels that he left at the edge of the shore. On his return, every eel had slithered over the side of the boat into the water and was gone.

May as well try to move her as Gull Rock: Gull Rock is part of the rocky ledge that lies off Lockeport Harbour.

Crazy as Luke's dog: someone who behaves as crazy as a dog that barks at the moon.

I'll fly aboard o' ye and dance a jig on yer palate: a raging threat, a tongue lashing.

Ah, da! Just growing up crows to peck their own eyes out: bringing up children without respect for their parents.

Born short and left over: people who are unable to provide the means for living.

He has the strength of a knot: this refers to a knot in a tree.

Pull your dory up alongside anytime: you are always welcome at our house.

Did something go down your Sunday throat: a crumb swallowed the wrong way.

It will never be seen on a trotting horse: an uneven hemline, for example, will never be seen when one is walking.

Look at that high stepper walking on eggshells: a young woman mincing along on high heels.

Pig when I leave, hog when I get home: how the story grew.

It's going round Robin Hood's barn: a rumour.

Running around Robbie Hunt's barn: getting nowhere.

Oh! I have a lump of location: I know where I'm going.

It never rains but it pours: for example, when an unexpected guest arrives, many more will follow.

He doesn't need to go all the way round Brown's barn to explain things to us: condemnation of a long sermon.

Long enough to go round Hyde Park: a long sermon.

Set down and tuck in: an invitation to dinner.

Driving his pigs to market: snoring.

Die the death of a woodpecker: to fall into a deep sleep from exhaustion.

Little pitchers have big ears: hears all the gossip.

Caught by the skin of the teeth: a narrow escape.

Trouble comes in threes: one misfortune will be followed by two more.

Bob White (or Jack Robinson) is out of jail: the big toe is through a hole in a sock.

A fly in the ointment: there's a problem somewhere.

A lick and a promise: light housekeeping.

Till the last gun fires: guests who stay late—until the last gun fires.

You're right on the bite today: have an answer for everything.

◆

An interesting way to call attention to a young girl's engagement ring is to say, "Seen anything of Pa's cows?" This is said with the ring finger at the corner of the mouth or on the forehead, imitating a young woman showing off her engagement ring, but pretending she's looking out the window for Pa's cows. Sometimes to the query, "Seen anything of Pa's cows?" is added, "Went away yesterday. Been gone a fortnight."

◆

Many sayings express opinions; others, appearance and character; some mental derangement or retardation. Some express disapproval; others offer advice. Some are exclamations and greetings. Whatever their meaning they are alive and add jest to conversation.

ADMONITION AND ADVICE

Think twice before you speak. Look twice before you leap.

Waste not, want not.

A stitch in time saves nine.

Cut your garment according to your cloth.

Mind your ways or you'll come out the little end of the horn.

Make hay while the sun shines.

A penny saved is as good as one earned.

Use your head to save your heels.

Keep your nose to the grindstone.

Don't put all your eggs in one basket.

A rolling stone gathers no moss.

CHARACTER

He has more gall than a brass monkey.

He's as brazen as they come.

He's as crooked as a ram's horn.

As slippery as an eel.

He's velvet smooth and not a wild turkey.

Not worth a hooraw in hell.

As independent as a hog on ice with his tail froze in.

He's as tough as a barrel of hammers.

Lazier than a home soldier. (During the war, a home soldier was a young man who did not enlist. It now refers to any young man inclined to be lazy.)

Fights like a bantam rooster.

I wouldn't give two cents and a button for him.

Sharp as a pin.

He'll sting yer quicker than Jerry paid the mortgage.

She can lie faster than a horse can trot.

He's going up fool's hill.

He's too big for his breeches.

As friendly as home-made apple pie.

PERSONAL APPEARANCE AND PERSONAL WORTH

A sight for sore eyes.

Thin as a pond loon. Thin as a crow. Stiff as a ramrod.

Pretty as a button. Pretty piece of calico.

Her eyes snap like a chipmunk's.

Looks like last year's bird's nest.

Looks like a birch broom in a fit.

As homely as a stump fence. Homely enough to stop a clock.

He's well thatched (plenty of hair). Head as thick as a pot.

She looks like a blueberry in a pan of skim milk.

MENTAL DERANGEMENT AND RETARDATION

She lacks all her buttons. She's off her rocker.

Wheels in her head.

Doesn't have two oars in the water. He rows with only one oar.

He doesn't play with a full pack.

He has a loose screw in the garret. Bats in the belfry.

Crazy as a bed bug. Silly as a coot. Gone cuckoo.

Feeble minded. Half nuts. Dim.

GOOD HEALTH

Fit as a fiddle.

Chipper.

Pink of condition.

Going strong.

POOR HEALTH
AND PHYSICAL DISABILITIES

Moger, a miserable, half-sick feeling.

Not fit for gull's bait.

Not feeling up to snuff.

Not feeling up to scratch.

Sick abed in the woodbox.

He's back up a bit.

He's run his course—his days are over.

Under the weather.

Just so-so.

One foot in the grave and the other all but.

He's having an off day.

Hauled out for repairs.

Fair to middling.

Deaf as a haddock.

MEANNESS

He'd skin a louse for its hide and tallow.

Mean enough to steal the pennies off a dead man's eyes.

As mean as all out doors.

POVERTY

Poorer than Job's tears. As poor as Job's turkey.

As poor as a church mouse.

Nip and tuck to make both ends meet.

As scarce as hen's teeth.

Live close to the bark. Live close to the bone.

Down to hard scratch.

GREETINGS

Hello, what's the price of hay?

It's a fine day for the race. What race? The human race.

Hi-yi! Hi-yi, sticky.

EXCLAMATIONS

Good day, Hessie.

Glory be to Betsy. Heavens to Betsy.

Shin bone of Hannah.

Holy mackerel. Holy mackinaw. Holy mister. Holy mister man. Gee, holy mister. Look ahere.

Boy, oh boy.

Gosh awful.

By golly.

Smokin' oakum.

Well, Jeely Crawley.

EXPRESSIONS

She was tickled pink.

Full tilt.

Every whip stitch.

Knuckle down.

Buckle to.

A dime a dozen.

Pretty penny.

Blue streak.

MISCELLANEOUS

She talks a blue streak.

Her tongue goes nine knots an hour.

Too many cooks spoil the broth.

The proof of the pudding is in the eating.

A new broom sweeps clean, but an old broom knows where to find the dirt.

Apple pie order.

As busy as nailers.

Strike while the iron's hot.

A bee in her bonnet. A flea in her ear.

Toe the mark.

Mind your Ps and Qs.

All wool and a yard wide.

As naked as a jay bird.

He swopped a devil for a witch.

Something or other splendid. That's something again.

He votes on the side the cookie crumbles.

Six of one, half a dozen of the other.

He can multiply a spade by a shovel and get a pick-axe.

He doesn't know beans when the bag's open.

He must have grown on a tree.

It's an ill wind turns none to good. It's an ill wind that blows no one any good.

It's cold enough for two pairs of braces.

A bad penny always returns.

As ignorant as Pat's pig.

First cousin to a sheep's head and that's all jaw.

I hope you live until a dead horse kicks your brains out.

That's a horse of another colour.

There's more than one way to kill a cat without choking it with butter.

SAYINGS

Everyone to his fancy and me to my Nancy, said the old man as he kissed the cow.

I'll be with you in two shakes of the old cow's tail, or, ten shakes of the old ram's tail.

I'm always behind, like the cow's tail.

A dog that will bring a bone will carry one away.

I don't want a dog to do my barking.

Can't teach an old dog new tricks.

Snug as a bug in a rug.

The luck of a lousy calf—live all winter, die in the spring.

Paying for a dead horse.

Just like picking fly specks out of pepper.

Whistling girls and crowing hens always come to some bad end.

As empty as last year's bird's nest.

Wouldn't that cramp your style.

All over creation and half the goose pasture.

Many who go for wool come back shorn.

Better half a loaf than no loaf at all.

A left-handed compliment.

It's a mile and a piece, and the piece is longer than the mile.

It cost an arm and a leg.

Ran like the dickens. Ran like Old Harry.

No nits, no lice.

Catch as catch can.

I'll be ready by seven or eleven.

Not right by a long shot.

Penny wise, pound foolish.

Wear at the toe, spend as you go.

Necessity is the mother of invention.

Neither proud nor particular.

Neither t'other nor which.

He who laughs last, laughs best.

It's time decent folks were in bed, and rogues and thieves jogging.

If you can't trust them alive, you can't trust them dead.

I heard by way of a slant.

I don't stay home sucking my thumb.

A fair-weather friend.

He bit off more than he could chew.

Dead as a door nail.

She's got the world on a string.

He's pushing up the daisies. Toes to roses.

Eat a peck and spew a bushel. (This is said of gulls.)

Slick as a whistle. Clean as a whistle.

Suffering like a lee thole pin.

The jig is up.

Fish or cut bait.

That won't skin his nose.

Didn't she set herself in a buttertub.

Pride must suffer pain. Pride goes before a fall.

The pot calling the kettle black.

Think twice before you speak.

Caps the climax.

Seven come eleven.

Lid off the pot.

It's better to be born lucky than rich.

Tempest in a teapot.

Swallows the driver and chases the horse.

Buttered both sides and jam in the middle.

Bump on a log.

Two heads are better than one.

An ounce of prevention is better than a pound of cure.

Nipped in the bud.

Long may your big jib draw.

Working straight out.

Birds of a feather flock together.

Let the cat out of the bag.

From the frying pan into the fire.

He bit off more than he could chew.

Everything comes in use once in seven years.

A mountain out of a mole hill.

Not many people get out of this world alive.

Don't count your chickens until they are hatched.

You can talk until the cows come home.

Talk is cheap.

Dragged through a knothole.

All good things come to an end.

Shoemaker stick to your last. Stick to your bush.

Cleanliness is next to Godliness.

HOME REMEDIES

No aspect of home folklore is recalled with greater delight than the old remedies that were part of one's childhood—a spoonful of a bitter tonic to freshen a sagging appetite or to purify the blood; a face washed with buttermilk; a plantain leaf bound over a bruised knee. Then there was the fun of gathering lichens—rock and tree cockles (barnacles), juniper berries, leaves of buca and broad-leaved plantain to be brewed into remedies and used as tradition decreed.

There were ways to cure illnesses, and there were ways to keep well. For good health, boughs of bayberry were brought into the house to ward off illness, or the dried leaves of bayberry were crushed and made into pillows. Then, as one woman wrote in her cookbook, "For good health—never eat Pork. Cook your beef very rare—the blood running out—and after eating take a glass of fruit juice to digest the meat quickly. Never eat Pork."

Many of the old names for illnesses have slipped into the past, remembered by only a few. A "breeding sore"—a sore that refused to heal and continued to breed—probably an old name for a skin cancer.

"Tissick," a lung condition that bordered on consumption, a word now supplanted by tuberculosis.

A "tissicky" cough, or a "real tissick cough" was a cause for grave concern.

A "milk leg," suffered by many women following childbirth, was believed to be caused by the milk from the breast flowing downward into the leg.

"Sprew" was another name for thrush—little white ulcers in the mouth.

"Titters" was a rash of tiny water blisters.

An "anger knot," "anger knob," and "anger ball" were names for a wen, especially one on a bald head. Children believed they are the curse of a bad temper, and that they, too, would grow an anger knot if they lost their temper.

"Moger" was an old word for feeling miserable.

Some of the following home cures are remedies of a century ago remembered by oldtimers in the 1930s; others are of a much later date recalled by those who brewed them as anxious young mothers. A few are still considered a good way to "backen" a cold, to ease a cough, to soothe a wasp's sharp sting.

ABSCESS

To draw an abscess to a head, a poultice was made of Surprise soap and brown sugar, or a leaf of a young cabbage was applied. The leaf was first heated before an open fire and wrapped round with a flannel to hold against the abscess.

AMPUTATION

When an arm or a leg had to be amputated there was great care taken that the part amputated was buried flat to prevent pain in a "phantom" arm or leg, from a bent finger or toe.

APPETIZERS

For a flagging appetite, a bitter tonic was made of august flowers, which it was also believed was strengthening, or one was brewed from juniper, or a quassia cup was filled with water and the bitter extract from the quassia wood was sipped from the cup.

On a card attached to a quassia cup used in Barrington was written:

"Quassia, a tropical American tree, derived its name from a Suriname Negro who used its bitter wood as a basis of a secret remedy. A drug extracted from it is used now as an appetizer, in dyspepsia, and as an insecticide."

"Those who owned the quassia cup poured water into it for a bitter drink to stimulate a sagging appetite." (As an insecticide, chips of quassia wood were boiled and used to wash the hair to kill head lice.)

ARTHRITIS

Arthritis was known as "rheumatism" and many of the old ways to prevent rheumatism are now used to "stave off" arthritis. *See* Rheumatism.

ASTHMA

For asthma, white-flowered jimson-weed, locally known as angel trumpets, was grown in an old garden in Cape Negro and the leaves dried and smoked for relief from asthma. Another old remedy was a jelly made from the flowers and seeds of sumac. They were steeped and the strained liquid used to make the jelly. An old cure for asthma, recommended by a doctor on Cape Island, was to walk barefoot in wet grass.

BANDAGES, COTTON BALLS, AND BABY POWDER

Bandages were made from long strips of cotton cut from a worn sheet and scorched in a hot oven until brown. Cotton balls, to be used when dressing wounds, were rolled from cotton batting used in the making of quilts and, like bandages, were scorched in a hot oven. Baby powder was made from flour scorched to a toasty brown.

BLADDER

The juice of the bunchberry plant was used for bladder and kidney infections. A present-day local remedy is cranberry juice.

TO PURIFY THE BLOOD

To be rid of impurities in the blood, every spring and fall a mixture of molasses and sulphur was taken. Someone who grew up in Clarks Harbour was given this remedy every fall when he was a little boy, to purify the blood and to thicken it for winter, "so you don't mind the cold so much." In Sandy Point, a father thought differently. He gave his little girl sulphur and molasses every spring "to thin the blood and get ready for summer." "If you thin the blood you don't mind the heat." The liquid from steeped red clover blossoms was taken to make good blood, as was the bitter syrup made from the roots of blackberries.

BLOOD PRESSURE

In Sandy Point, a remedy for high blood pressure was cranberry juice.

BOILS

To draw a boil to a head, equal parts of hard soap and sugar were applied as a plaster. Cow-dung poultices were also used, as was the inside of a fig, both of which had "painful drawing powers."

BRONCHITIS

A mixture of molasses and soda was taken to relieve the congestion of bronchitis. Another remedy was to pour hot tea over a teaspoonful of honey and add the juice of half a lemon.

BURNS AND BRUISES

For a burn, the white of an egg, or the inside coating of the shell of a raw egg drawn from the shell, was used to exclude the air and to soothe the stinging pain. Bruises were rubbed with a soothing salve and covered with a plantain leaf.

CANCER

The juice steeped from clover leaves was used for stomach cancer.

CANKERS

The root of gold thread was steeped and used as a mouthwash for cankers.

CARING FOR THE SICK

When caring for the sick, especially one suffering from a cold and a sore throat, a clove was held in the mouth, as a preventative measure.

CHILBLAINS

For chilblains, the feet were soaked in salt and water, and oil was poured over the sores to soothe the burning itch. Or, the feet were soaked in warm water to which turpentine had been added. Sometimes chilblains were rubbed with a hog's bladder dipped in turpentine or with a piece of chalk dipped in vinegar.

CHILDBIRTH

During birth of a baby a mother was attended by a midwife, a "granny"; a doctor was called to the bedside only in an emergency. To hasten and to ease the pain of childbirth, tansy tea was given to the mother when the baby was ready to be born. In Shag Harbour, a young mother lying in bed following the birth of her baby was given a decoction of steeped "pissabeds" (dandelions) to provoke the flow of urine. When a mother suffered a milk leg (*phlegmasia alba dolens*), believed to be caused by the milk from her breast flowing downward into her leg, she was kept in bed by her midwife for many days, sometimes weeks, lying flat on her back, her leg lifted on pillows.

CHILL

For a chill, hot buttered rum was administered, made of brown sugar and butter and a noggin of rum in hot water. A school teacher in Barrington recorded in her diary in the 1830s that for a chill she took some warm peppermint tea and got into bed surrounded with bottles of hot water.

CHAPPED HANDS

Chapped hands were rubbed with mutton fat or tallow, or they were washed with soft soap, the soap carefully washed from the skin and the hands rubbed with white sugar.

CHOKING

When a crumb went down the wrong way, the shoulders were patted vigorously at the back of the neck to dislodge the crumb.

COLDS

Among the many home cures for colds were those to "ward off" a cold and those "to backen" a cold.

To "ward off" a cold, a piece of camphor was hung around the neck or carried in a pocket, or a clove was held in the mouth. Honey was considered good to ward off a cold, as was cod liver oil and the juice of citrus fruit. Hot ginger tea was used to guard against a cold following a chill.

To "backen" a cold, a drink of hot lemonade and soaking one's feet in a bucket of hot ginger or hot mustard water were recommended. Either the chest was rubbed vigorously with hot grease and covered with flannel, or a hot mustard poultice was applied.

For a cold that refused to "backen," drinking hot mint tea and binding a salt herring or a piece of salt pork around the neck would draw the fever from the cold.

Another way was to dip mullein leaves in vinegar and bind the leaves to the soles of the feet. To break her cold, one woman remembered her aunt in Allendale made her sit behind a hot base-burner with a piece of salt pork rolled in a woolen cloth bound around her neck, and half a barrel top, burning hot, pressed against her back. Another way to break a stubborn cold was to get into a tub of hot water laced with a generous portion of soda, then into a warm bed with a tumbler of rum to drink, mixed with brown sugar, lemon juice and hot water.

For a chest cold that refused to "backen," an old woman in Doctor's Cove cut a large heart of greased brown paper and stuck it to her granddaughter's chest. A similar cure was used in North East Harbour where the chest was rubbed with hot grease and covered with a piece of brown paper folded and cut to fit around the neck and over the chest, for, "There's nothing like brown paper to keep out the cold and keep in the heat." Onion poultices were also used for a mulish chest cold as was a plaster made of mustard, Indian corn meal, and vinegar spread on linen and applied between the shoulders, back and front.

CONSUMPTION

For consumption (tuberculosis), a dreaded disease that invaded many homes less than a century ago, an old remedy was made of yarrow tea with drops of spruce sap, seven drops to a spoonful of the tea.

An old remedy remembered in Lockeport was to drink melted tallow and sleep outdoors in winter and summer. Others went into a pine forest and lived in a tent.

On Cape Island, a doctor considered buttermilk and sleeping outdoors as the best cure for consumption.

CORNS

To ease the pain of corns, the feet were soaked in a pan of water, then olive oil was applied. Corns and calluses were also rubbed with Minard's liniment.

COUGHS

Homemade cough remedies were made from the buds of balm of Gilead (balsam poplar), from boneset (thoroughwort) steeped and mixed with molasses. Black rock lichen and rock polypody boiled in water and added to molasses made a good cough mixture. Lemon juice, cream and molasses, or ginger and molasses, also provided relief from a cough. The juice from a raw onion, a raw sliced onion sprinkled with sugar, and onions boiled in molasses and butter, with vinegar or a few drops of kerosene were three ways to soothe a racking cough.

A cough remedy brewed by an esteemed doctor of Cape Island was made of a base of boiled Irish moss, to which was added cod liver oil and a generous spoonful of checkerberry (wintergreen), for flavouring.

For a vigorous cough medicine, Minard's liniment in molasses, or molasses and "pepper sass," concocted from red peppers boiled in vinegar, were used.

CRAMPS

The old standby for stomach cramps was hot Jamaica ginger. To ward off this complaint, a cramp knot (a tree knot) was carried in a pocket.

CROUP

A few drops of Friar's Balsam on a lump of sugar was used for croup and goose grease was rubbed on the chest.

A dry mustard poultice made by smearing lard on a cloth and rubbing in dry mustard was used by a woman in Green Harbour. For her grandson she made a flannel vest buttoned up the back to keep him from having the croup.

In Lockeport, an old way to relieve croup was to bind a salt herring to the sole of each foot.

CUTS AND BLEEDING WOUNDS

For cuts and bleeding wounds, brown paper was held over the cut, and the lining from an egg shell was used as an adhesive to hold together the edges of the wound. To stop bleeding, thick, grey cobwebs from a haymow were bound over the wound, and sphagnum moss or flour were used to clot the blood. A lotion to stop bleeding was brewed from balm of Gilead, from tansy, from burdock leaves, or chockberries. Mutton tallow was sometimes applied to the wound, and a plantain, burdock, or tansy leaf was bound over the wound.

DIARRHOEA

For diarrhoea, steeple bush (hardhack) was mixed with boiled milk as a hot drink. Many shy away from the word diarrhoea. One man said, "I had the run out." To two little boys, it was "the flying axe handles."

DIPHTHERIA

For diphtheria there were only two ways to hopefully prevent this dreaded disease. "Campfire" (camphor) in a little bag was hung around the neck, or, in its absence, tobacco. A more stringent method was to gargle with kerosene.

DISINFECTANTS

When neighbours returned to their homes after helping in a house infected with a contagious disease, they plunged their clothing into a tub of boiling hot water and creosote. Following the death of a person from an infectious disease, the home was fumigated with burning sulphur.

DYSENTERY

For dysentery, finely-chopped mutton simmered in new milk, with brandy, cinnamon and sugar, was taken by the glassful two or three times a day. Sometimes just warm milk was given to soothe the intestinal tract and quiet the stomach.

EARACHE

To ease an earache, pieces of hot baked onion were inserted in the ear, or warm olive oil was poured into the ear passage.

In Barrington Passage, a woman used to ease her daughter's earache by filling a small flannel bag with coarse salt, heating it in the oven, and pressing the bag against the painful ear. Another remedy was to pour hot water over hops, then place the hops in a bag to hold against the ear.

ERYSIPELAS

This red and painful inflammation of the skin was relieved with a poultice of cranberries.

EYES

Sore eyes and inflamed eyelids were bathed with a weak solution of borax. Dirt beneath the eyelid was removed by inserting a flax seed beneath one corner of the eyelid. As it worked across the eyeball, beneath the eyelid, the dirt was pushed out of the corner of the eye. Another way was to pinch the eyelid and draw it forward, at the same time, blowing the nose vigorously.

FEVERS

A bitter drink was taken to break a fever, or hot boiled burdock leaves were bound to the sole of each foot.

For a malarial fever, a Barrington sea captain recorded in his ship's log in the 1850s that a doctor recommended an active purge, followed by "quinine in powder till the patient feels his head snap and crack."

FINGER SUCKING

It was considered a disaster for a baby to suck the index finger, for the bone would be softened and the finger twisted. To stop finger sucking, a leaf of wormwood was bound to the finger, or the finger was rubbed with wormwood leaving a bitter taste.

CHARM FOR A FOOT GONE TO SLEEP

Dip finger in water and make a cross on the toe of your shoe. When the cross has dried, your foot will awake.

'FLU

During a 'flu epidemic in 1918, the school children in Sandy Point were given a square of camphor in a bag to hang around their necks.

FRECKLES

Buttermilk was used to make freckles disappear.

GALL BLADDER

For gall bladder trouble, a spoonful of olive oil was taken every morning.

GOUT

Canned cherries were taken for the relief of gout.

GUM BOILS

For gum boils, a wet finger was dipped in powdered alum and rubbed over the boil. To stop bleeding, strips of brown paper were pressed against them.

HEADACHE

A tight band was bound around the head to ease a headache, or mullein leaves dipped in vinegar, or fresh poppy leaves were applied to the forehead.

Someone on Cape Island had a piece of camphor in a bottle of rum to rub on an aching forehead.

HEART TROUBLE

A Shelburne doctor told a patient with a weak heart, who could not walk uphill without breathlessness, to walk up the hill backwards.

HICCOUGHS

A little white sugar, or sugar and lemon juice, was held in the mouth to control hiccoughs. Babies were given a little sugar in water. Another remedy was to hold a paper bag over the head.

HIVES

Raw onions were eaten to cure hives.

INDIGESTION

Hot peppermint tea and hot Jamaica ginger were sipped for indigestion—"to bring up the gas."

INFECTIONS

Turpentine was the stand-by to combat infection, and a wounded foot or hand was soaked in a tub of hot water and turpentine.

INSECT BITES

A woman in Port La Tour discovered that "Fuller's earth is excellent for the bites of black flies."

For bee and wasp strings, a pack of black mud was wrapped over the swelling or it was rubbed with black swamp muck. Flea bites were bathed with soda water.

ITCH

For the itch, rum and sulphur were mixed into a paste, rubbed on one night and washed off the next.

KIDNEY TROUBLE

A decoction made from steeped juniper berries was used for kidney trouble. For the retention of urine, tea made from august flowers, dandelions, or the leaves of buca or foxberry, local names for bearberry that grows in abundance on the dry barren lands of Shelburne County, provoked the flow of urine. When these failed, steeped pumpkin seeds provided a remedy that "saved a doctor's bill and even helped a horse."

LAME BACK AND SORE MUSCLES

A soothing lotion was brewed from the branches and berries of juniper to be used on a lame back and for sore muscles, and the juice boiled from juniper berries was used as a medicine to ease the same pain. Sea water was rubbed on muscles to relieve stiffness.

LAXATIVES

A woman who lived in North East Harbour remembered that when her brother suffered a painful bowel disorder, one of the local doctors told her father to dig up rhubarb root, which her mother steeped, making a drink for the patient. Later, the juice was mixed with flour and the boy ate it. "There's nothing better than rhubarb to soothe the bowels."

Few of the home cures were used as frequently as home-brewed laxatives, either rhubarb root or sulphur and molasses. As diets were conducive to constipation, being "bound up" was often feared, and laxatives were sometimes taken daily for a good "cleaning out." For a gentle purge, a large handful of checkerberry (wintergreen) and a handful of sarsaparilla leaves were boiled for five minutes in a quart of water. A small tumblerful taken every two hours, with fruit juice between times would "assist the operation."

LIVER AND LIVER PINS

There was an old belief that the liver is held in place by "liver pins," and a sudden jolt would displace the pins and the liver would protrude as an ugly lump. To maintain a healthy liver, a bitter tonic was made of august flowers (fall dandelions) and the bitters were kept warm in a pitcher perched on the high oven of the old Niagara stove.

MEASLES

To bring out the measles a bitter drink was administered, such as bayberry bark steeped in water, or a summer savory tea. If these failed, the measles were "forced out" with hot tea made of nanny tassels (sheep dung) brewed and strained through a sieve.

MENSTRUATION

For menstruation, "If you are late in coming around, steep some tansy and drink it."

MOUTHWASHES

A mouthwash to swab a baby's tender mouth was made from wild rose petals boiled and sweetened with a little sugar, or a mild wash was made from gold thread. Blackberry and raspberry leaves were steeped for mouthwashes, and someone in Allendale made a gargle for a sore mouth from strong tea and alum.

NERVOUS DISORDERS

For nervous disorders, wild sarsaparilla was brewed and made into a drink.

NOSEBLEED

To stop a nosebleed, brown paper was pressed between the teeth and upper lip, the head bent backward, and cold water applied to the back of the neck.

PILES

Old remedies for piles were to rub them with oakum, or to sit in a pan of hot salt water.

PIMPLES

Pimples were rubbed with lard.

PINGEONS

A Sandy Point fisherman remembered that, "Eight turns of a brass chain are worn around the wrists" by the Bank fishermen to prevent "pingeons."

To prevent these painful white sores caused by salt water and the chafing of oilskins against the wrist, inshore fishermen wound yarn around the wrists or wore "wristers" knit of white yarn. For a cure, pingeons were "treated" with kerosene or creosote.

POISON IVY

In Shelburne, for the painful burning of the skin from contact with poison ivy, the leaves of the sweet fern were steeped in water to bathe on the infected area. Naphtha was also applied.

PNEUMONIA

To ward off pneumonia, a piece of red flannel tied around the chest, or a red flannel vest was worn. If red flannel failed and congestion developed in the lungs, hot onion or hot bread poultices were bound across the chest and back and covered with a heavy woolen vest. A more stringent method was a mustard plaster made of flour and mustard mixed to a stiff paste and spread between layers of cloth and bound over the chest and back. To soothe the burning flesh when the plaster was removed the chest and back were rubbed with goose grease or sweet olive oil.

RHEUMATISM

Scotch broom steeped in turpentine was an old home cure for rheumatism and was applied to stiff, aching joints and muscles.

Many remember one way to prevent rheumatism was to carry a knurl or knot cut from a spruce tree, and to ease the pain and stiffness in the hands, a knot cut from a spruce tree, known as a "cramp knot," was squeezed in the hands. Others carried a potato or chestnut in a pocket to ward off rheumatism or arthritis, or wore a brass chain around an ankle or a wrist.

Someone in Baccaro wore a slice of potato sewn in a small bag around her neck to ease the pain. Others wrapped a slice of potato around each foot to relieve arthritis in the legs, or slept with a potato at the foot of the bed to take away all diseases as well as arthritis.

RINGWORM AND RING-AROUND

Ringworm scabs were painted with iodine. Ring-around, a painful infection around the finger nail, was soaked in hot water and a soothing ointment applied.

SALT RHEUM

This irritation of the skin, especially of the hands and fingers, was believed to be caused by eating hot oatmeal every day for breakfast. Being too hot for the blood, the cure was to stop eating oatmeal!

SHINGLES

The best known remedy for shingles was application of cornstarch.

SMELLING SALTS

Smelling salts were made by pouring vinegar or rum over camphor in a bottle.

THE SNIFFING BOWL

The sniffing bowl was used for preparing hot steaming brandy which was inhaled to clear the nasal passages.

SORES AND TITTERS

Titters, very fine water blisters caused by irritation of the skin, were bathed with a soothing lotion made from the bark of hackmatack. For sores and pimples, salves were made from the buds of balm of Gilead boiled in water and added to mutton tallow or hog lard, stirred until thick and strained through a woolen cloth.

In Sable River, a similar salve was made from beeswax, mutton tallow and leeks, and as part of the healing process a plantain leaf was bound over the sore.

A very good Micmac remedy for a sore was the sap squeezed from the blisters of balsam fir.

SORE MOUTH

A sore mouth was rinsed with mouthwashes made from rose petals, from the roots of gold thread, and from blackberry and raspberry leaves.

SORE THROAT

For a sore throat, goose grease and pepper were applied to a piece of flannel and tied as a bandage around the neck, and for a quincy sore throat, a slice of salt herring or salt pork wrapped in flannel was bound around the throat to draw the fever from the infection. Another cure for a sore throat was to bind around the throat an old woolen sock turned wrong side out.

Gargles for a sore throat were made from salt, vinegar, and water. Steeped gold thread made a soothing gargle, as did a mixture of strong tea and alum. As well as gargles, there was a mixture to be taken by the spoonful made from cayenne peppers, black pepper and fine salt bruised together, beaten into a paste and mixed with boiling hot water. It was then strained, added to vinegar and bottled for future use.

SPRAINS

Tansy soaked in vinegar was bound over a sprain, or mullein leaves were made into a poultice and wrapped about the injured joint, or the sprain was rubbed with camphor gum dissolved in rum. A sprained ankle was known as a "turned ankle."

STOMACH DISORDERS

The liquid from steeped ground juniper and from boiled boneset (thoroughwort) relieved stomach distress, and camomile tea eased indigestion. Two or three teaspoonfuls of liquid from steeplebush (hardhack) mixed with boiled milk were taken hot to ease stomach disorders.

STYES

Styes on the eyelids were rubbed with vaseline.

SUMMER COMPLAINT

With the hot, muggy days of summer, diarrhoea and an upset stomach were common complaints. A cup of warm milk eased the disorder, followed by a light diet.

SWELLINGS

Tansy steeped in vinegar was used for swellings, and a potato poultice was used for swollen feet and ankles.

THRUSH

A mouthwash made of gold thread was used for the little white ulcers in the mouth known as sprew or thrush.

TONICS

Homemade tonics provided pep and energy, and were used to purify the blood, and to revive a lost appetite. For a spring tonic, tansy tea, or tansy steeped in molasses, were favourites.

In Allendale, a tonic was made of august flowers brewed with cherry bark, princess pine, ground hemlock and checkerberry (wintergreen), with red clover blossoms thrown in for good blood.

Steeped wormwood with raisins provided a good year-round tonic, and mandrake bitters were used as a tonic for the liver. Sarsaparilla was considered a good tonic, as was boneset, which was boiled for a stomach tonic.

A concoction of burdock steeped and boiled with raisins was administered by an old man in Barrington to his grandchildren every spring to rid the blood of an accumulation of impurities.

On Cape Island, a healthful drink for children was made from the bark of white alder, gold thread, sarsaparilla, and the leaves of Labrador tea steeped together, sweetened with molasses and boiled down to a syrup to be mixed with water.

TOOTHACHE AND TOOTH CARE

There were numbers of old ways to ease the pain of an aching tooth. Where there was a cavity, creosote (chimney soot) was wedged into the hollow, and for aching teeth, perfume and shaving lotion and even Minard's liniment were used. One remedy considered of special merit was a mixture of vinegar, spirits and a teaspoon of salt held in the mouth.

Soda and salt were used to brush the teeth, and dry toast was considered excellent to remove tartar from the teeth.

TYPHOID FEVER

In Sable River, wormwood was given for typhoid fever.

WARTS

To cure warts, one suggestion was to steal a piece of meat, rub it on the warts and as the meat dried, the warts would disappear. Better still, have someone steal the meat, rub it over the warts and bury it in an unknown plot of ground. For a facial wart, have a friend rub it with a slice of raw apple.

Another way, remembered by someone who grew up on the Hawk, was to cut a potato in two, rub each half over the warts, then carefully join the potato together and bury it. As the potato rotted, the warts vanished. "Nobody ever said what would happen if the potato grew."

Besides stolen meat, apples and potatoes, cards were efficacious. A little girl in Shelburne rubbed a wart on one of her fingers with a Christmas card and threw the card in the street. Whoever picked it up would get the wart and her's would drop off. For days she watched. At last an old man came along the street and picked up the card and she shouted joyfully, "There goes my wart." She gave it a flick with her thumbnail and it dropped off.

Fishermen wash their warts in the water left in the hollow of a rock as the tide falls on the dark of the moon.

CHARMS FOR WARTS

In Sandy Point, an elderly woman charmed warts from a friend's hands by marking a cross with chalk on each wart, and for each one she cut a cross in the soot of a stove cover. As the crosses burned in the soot, the warts disappeared. This was done in silence, not a word spoken to break the charm—"And there were forty warts and two women!"

"They all came off," the old lady reported proudly. "She said I did her a great favour."

To be rid of her warts, a woman of Brass Hill went out in the field on a night of the new moon, knelt down and pulled a handful of grass and threw it over her left shoulder toward the moon, saying, "New moon I'm seeing, warts a-fleeing." When she reached into the grass for a second handful, her fingers closed over a toad. As everyone knows, handling toads gives warts!

There were those who professed to be wart-charmers and went from town to town. One of these came to Shelburne. A little girl whose hands and wrists were covered with warts went to him. He rubbed them with his hands, chanting as he did so. The next day at school her seatmate could find no trace of the warts.

WHOOPING COUGH

For whooping cough, an old remedy was raw sliced onions sprinkled with sugar.

WORMS

The old belief that every child who looked peaked (thin and sickly) had worms was the bane of childhood. To be "rid" of worms, their mothers concocted potions of wormwood and molasses, steeped tansy leaves, and gave them the ground roes of kiacks, mixed with eggshells in jelly, "to cut the heads right off of 'um."

Another way to rid a peaked-looking child of worms was to bind a sack of wormwood around the lower abdomen.

To entice a tapeworm into the open, the victim was starved for three or four days. Then a bowl of milk was placed beside the patient's bed. "The worm will be so hungry, he will come right out to drink the milk."

WOUNDS

From the sap of balsam fir mixed with yolks of fresh eggs was made a salve used for green wounds. For a wound suspected to have "poison" in it, steeped tansy was made into a lotion to bathe the wound.

TO WARD OFF WINTER ILLNESSES

In Sandy Point, women gathered bayberry in the fall and kept it in the house during the winter, to ward off winter illnesses.

WEATHER LORE

*F*rom years of watching the changing patterns of the clouds, the silk of the spiders' webs, and listening to the sound of surf on the shore, has been gathered the wisdom of weather lore, along with rhymes and sayings, interwoven with superstitions.

SIGNS OF AN APPROACHING STORM

A "land loom" appears before a storm. "Loom" is a sailor's word for the appearance of a distant ship that is "looming," as if lifted above the surface of the sea. A land loom is a shimmering veil of blue and grey on the horizon above which the land appears, as if lifted above the surface of the sea. Sometimes the land mass lifted above the sea is dark and ominous. Two locations in Shelburne County are noted for the appearance of this mirage—the long, slender point of Baccaro, and the rocks and lighthouse of Gull Rock off the shores of Lockeport. Known as a land loom along Cape Sable shores, along the eastern shores of the county it is "land out of water."

A "glin" is a bright gleam of sunshine in a bank of fog.

It gives meaning to the old saying on the shores of Cape Sable that "a southern glin for a wet skin." East of Cape Sable, in the Carleton Village-Roseway area, where the word used is "glen," it is an "eastern glen wets your skin." A glen is a strip of clear sky in the east, lying on the horizon between the sea and dark clouds above. Glin and glen suggest words from German and Swedish sources, from "*glinmern*," to gleam, and "*gleinma*," as used in "a gleinma of light" for that first gleam of light at daybreak.

♦

There are many signs of rain and wind in the offing, and of storms at sea. A glassy sea in the early morning streaked with oily yellow soon brews a storm, and a glassy sky at daybreak foretells a nearby storm. A heavy ground swell, the heaving upward of the sea from beneath the surface of the water, is a clue to storms out at sea that have sent swelling billows towards the land. When long sunbeams, like the spokes of a mighty wheel, reach down from the sun, there will be rain, for the sun is "drawing water" upward from the earth into the sky to fill the rain clouds. A gleaming sundog to the south of the sun foretells a storm from the south; a sundog to the north, a storm from the north. When halos, or rings around the sun, lessen in size there will be a storm within twenty-four hours.

♦

As the sea and the sky foretell future weather, there are other signs of an approaching storm or of days of fine weather, and folk beliefs and sayings.

If spider webs are heavy with dew drops in the early morning, it will be a fine day; but if rain drops cling to window sashes and to the slender branches of shrubs and leaves following a shower, there will be more rain.

When pots boil dry and sparks from the fire, called "wild geese" or "soldiers," march in the soot of stove covers and in the soot of fireplaces, it will soon rain. Cats are playful when a storm is brewing; when they wash behind their ears, rain is in the offing; and, the wind the following day will blow from whichever direction the cat's tail points when asleep. For a rooster to fly to the top rail of a fence and crow is a sure sign of rain. A storm is on its way inland when sea birds fly close to the shore and hover in sheltered coves. When a lone gull cries at night there will be a storm.

◆

There are other old beliefs and sayings about the weather: rain before seven, stop before eleven; between twelve and two the weather will decide what it will do; and the weather will change with the turn of the tide. Friday is the fairest or the foulest, and a clear sunset on Friday—rain by Sunday.

If a patch of blue sky glimpsed behind broken rain clouds is big enough to make a Dutchman a pair of pantaloons or a sailor a pair of pants the rain will drift away. Then, "a sunshiny shower won't last an hour," but "sunshiny showers" brew three days of showers. Such showers tell that the devil is beating his wife. "Poor Soul! What an old devil he is!"

When the rain comes pelting down, it is said to be "raining cats and dogs" or "pitchforks and barn shovels." Then, as the rain lessens, and the wind moderates, it is "piping down." A very fine cloudless day is humbly accepted as a "weather breeder," for the good Lord cannot be expected to send two such fine days in a row. There is a strange superstition that to boldly assume tomorrow will be fine will bring a storm.

Red skies are significant to those who watch the sunrise and the sunset, for:

Evening red and morning grey,
That's the sign of a bonny day;
Evening grey and morning red,
The ewe and her lamb will go wet to bed.

In Green Harbour, their rhymes express the same weather wisdom.

Evening red, morning grey,
Sets the traveller on his way;
Evening grey, morning red,
Brings the rain on our heads.

TO CHANGE THE WEATHER

To change the weather turn a dead snake on its back. If sunny, it will rain; if raining, it will clear. Others say to turn a snake belly-up will always bring rain. To change the direction from which the wind is blowing, hang a dead snake in the corner of the room from which direction you want the wind to blow. On a very calm day, to bring a little wind to limp sails, stand before the mast and whistle gently.

DAYS AND SIGNS THAT FORETELL FUTURE WEATHER

Certain days are believed to foretell future weather. The first twelve days of the new year determine the weather of the twelve months ahead, each day representing the pattern of weather for each month. In October, the last three days of the month indicate the weather during the winter; the direction of the wind when the spring sun crosses "the line"—the equinox—determines the weather for the summer. St. Swithin's Day and Ground Hog Day are watched for the weather in the days to come. If it rains on St. Swithin's Day, it will rain for forty days; if the ground hog sees his shadow, there will be six more weeks of winter. If the day is dark and he is not frightened by his shadow, the back of the winter is broken.

An abundance of berries on mountain ash (dogwood), and on the shrubs of bayberry and Canada holly, are signs of a heavy, long winter when the birds will need many berries to survive; few berries clinging to trees as fall comes to a close betoken a mild winter. Robins that linger late in the fall, as worms remain near the surface of the ground, and caterpillars do not seek shelter are interpreted as signs of a gentle winter.

FOG LORE

There are many ways to speak of the density and motion of fog. A "scud of fog" tells of light wisps of fog scudding in from the sea. An old captain of Sandy Point watched as the fluffs of fog passed the setting sun, and commented, "Perhaps the moon will scoff it off."

A "fog-eater" is the sun itself when it dries the moisture from a bank of fog; it "eats a peck and spews a bushel." A dry fog holds little moisture and lingers over the land as "fog mull," resembling the thin veils of mull once fashionable on ladies' hats.

Some refer to fog as "she." A low-lying fog bank hanging over the sea in which boats are soon lost to view is a "dungeon of fog." A young man remembers when fishing in a dungeon of fog, he had to light a lamp to repair the engine, and glancing back, he saw his shadow against the fog.

As a land loom distorts the land, a "fog loom" distorts buildings and ships, giving them a strange, mysterious appearance. A "fog breeze" brings fog in over the land from the sea, where it lingers as a "smother of fog"; when the fog leaves the land and goes to sea, rain will follow the fog. It is said, "a winter fog will freeze a dog," for a foggy day in winter soon turns cold.

◆

When the fog was heavy over the land, "a real coarse fog," a woman, who lived in a lighthouse, remembered her mother holding their cat in a corner of their living room to entice the wind to blow the fog away. Another way to shift the fog from the land was to burn an old shoe, running with the shoe around the four corners of the house, muttering strange incantations as it was thrown over the right shoulder. If the old shoe failed, there was, yet again, the cat. Tie it in a box and place the box at the corner of the house from whence the wind must blow to lift the fog from the land.

CLOUDS AND SKY

"Smerry" or "smurry" refers to a light scum of clouds that look as if a storm is brewing. Sometimes the words is "smeary" as if from "smear," and in Clarks Harbour one person spoke of a "smeary sky" as "smeerry." "Goat's hair" are fine, hair-like clouds. "Mare's tails" are long wisps of clouds that "make tall ships carry short sail." A "mackerel sky" is streaked with mottled clouds, suggesting the colour and appearance of a mackerel and signifies "not twenty-four hours dry."

"Muggy" weather is "warm and unelastic," and a stiff breeze is required to whirl it away, or a "tempest," as a thunderstorm is called. "Lawery" weather is heavy with overcast dark clouds threatening or agitating a storm.

WIND

There are "smokey sou'westers" and "dry easterlys" that never brew a shower of rain. For the weather to clear during a storm the wind must "haul" through the south into the west; if it "backs in," or "backens," through the north into the west, the weather will again "thicken up" because the wind has gone against the sun and it will soon swing back into the east. An "in" wind is one that has hauled into the west or north; an "out" wind has backed into the south or east. "When the wind comes around a bit," it will clear; if it continues to come round into the west, the weather will remain fine. Sometimes the wind "goes round the compass" as it whirls around or "baffles."

On a "lur'd day," when the wind is from the leeward, men that fished from small sail boats and depended upon a favourable wind to carry them off shore, would plant their potatoes or mend their fences.

On a windy day, if the lower clouds break into small clouds, the wind will moderate; if the heavy clouds break, the wind will die down and the weather will clear. When birds suddenly change direction in flight, they turn to the direction from which the wind will shift its course. Sometimes a bad wind storm turns out to be less severe than expected and "we don't get the hef of it"; sometimes it hits "butt end fo'most." If the wind goes down with the sun "trust it not for again it will run." It's "airin' up" is another way of saying it's "blowing up" a breeze; a "scoffer" is a wind that will scoff the clouds away. Hurricanes brewed in the south give August twisters and September gales, and winds from the south give "line gales" when the sun crosses the line at the spring equinox.

◆

An old rhyme learned by a Cape Island fisherman when he was a little boy declares the wind's temperament.

When the wind is in the north,
Then the traveller may go forth.
When the wind is in the south,
It blows the bait into the fish's mouth.
When the wind is in the west,
Then the weather is always best.
When the wind is in the east,
It's neither good for man nor beast.

SNOW

The first flakes of snow measure the storm to follow: large, wet flakes soon melt against the earth; tiny, firm pellets and flakes build into a heavy snowfall. As fine flakes of snow foretell a heavy fall of snow, when the wind is blowing northeast and the woods are "shiny," snow is on its way. The "robin's snow" that comes late in the spring following the arrival of the first robins, is nature's way to moisten the earth and entice the worms upward into the waiting beaks of the robins.

FROST

In the fall, three mornings of frost will bring rain to the earth. Frost on the pine trees, when it melts quickly, brings rain; when it melts slowly, there will be snow.

When there is blowing frost on a winter day, there will be a snowstorm.

ICE

When ponds are frozen with ice and water rises over the ice, and when rocks are frozen over with ice under a stream of water, soft weather is on its way.

After the ice has broken in cakes from the shore, "ice weather" still clings to the land, believed to be generated by icebergs still lying off the coast of Cape Breton.

NORTHERN LIGHTS

Northern lights flickering against the winter sky foretell soft weather, a thaw and rain.

THUNDER

A tempest, a thunderstorm, not only clears the weather, but a fall tempest means a mild winter; a spring tempest, a cool summer.

MOON AND STARS

When there are many stars shining in the night sky, there will be a storm: rain in the summer, and in the winter, snow before morning; a few stars, fine weather. In late August when the Milky Way, the Milkmaid's Path, lies closest to the earth and is seen throbbing with light in the clear night sky, there will be an early frost. A single star near the moon as it glides across the sky denotes a nearby storm. A star following the full moon—a big ship towing a little boat—a wind-storm brewing; a star ahead of the moon—a little boat towing a big ship—fair weather.

The weather on the first day of the new moon is significant. If it rains on the first day of the new moon it will rain for three days. A dry new moon lies on its back and holds the water that would otherwise fall as rain to the earth, and a wet new moon stands upright in the sky, so that the water falls to the earth; if slightly tipped backward and a powder horn could hang on the sharp tip of the moon, the weather will be fine until the storm of the full moon. A ring around the moon a storm soon; two stars within the ring there will be a storm in two days. If a single star can be seen, the storm is one day away; no star, the storm will break before the light of day.

No one remembers why "Saturday's moon comes seven years too soon."

RAINBOWS

Rainbows are watched for the weather lore expressed in the old rhyme:

Rainbow at night,
Sailors delight;
Rainbow in the morning,
Sailors take warning.

◆

To know weather lore is to do as the old fisherman of Cape Island said, "It aired up to the north and blew black, and this pilgrim stayed on shore."

BIRD LORE

About birds have been woven superstitions and weather lore, and names of significance, some local, some more general.

For a bird to flutter about a window or even fly close to a window is a warning of impending disaster; for a bird to fly boldly into a house there will be a death in the family. The plaintive *coo-coo-coo* of the Black-billed Cuckoo is believed to be a harbinger of illness and death in a community. To see Mother Carey's chickens (Leach's Storm Petrel) is a bad omen. They are evil, and are called "devil birds," or "witch birds." Swallows are bad luck, especially when they circle around a house where someone is ill. Kill a swallow and the cows will give bloody milk. A death will follow when a bird is willfully killed at sea.

Birds are watched for signs of future weather, and for signs that a storm will soon be over. When gulls fly high overhead in slow widening circles there will be days of blue sky and sunshine; when they fly low over the land, a storm is in the offing. Seabirds, when they fly inshore to sheltered coves and inlets, are harbingers of a storm moving inland from the sea; when they begin to fly seaward, the storm will soon ebb. Noisy Blue Jays are forerunners of a storm not twenty-four hours away. And when a rooster flies to the top rail of a fence and crows, he is asking for rain. On dry summer days when robins murmur a soft pleading cry, it is for rain to moisten the earth and entice the worms upward into their waiting beaks. When owls call in the night, a storm is on its way.

CROWS

A flock of crows is counted one by one with the old rhyme:

One crow sorrow.
Two crows joy,
Three crows a letter,
Four crows a boy.
Five crows silver,
Six crows gold,
Seven crows a secret,
Eight crows told.

A variant of this old rhyme says:

Three crows a wedding,
Four crows a boy; ...
Seven crows a secret never to be told.

If someone is with you when you see one crow, the curse is broken; if alone, to break the curse, spit over your left shoulder, or say:

One crow sorrow,
Kiss your hand and give it a toss;
And wish a wish
To take your sorrow away.

For a crow to fly over the bow of a fish boat when pushing off shore, the boat must be turned back to the land and the ritual of starting a voyage repeated. For one crow to fly over the roof of a house is bad luck; two crows flying together over the roof will bring happiness. To shoot a crow will bring bad luck tumbling your way.

◆

In stories, loons and gulls, mate for life. When one loses its mate, it goes off to a lonely shore of a lonely lake apart from others it has known. Its wild, lonely cry expresses its sadness, and awareness of an approaching storm.

NAMES OF BIRDS

"Alderbird" is the Yellow Warbler that builds its nest in alders.

"Blossombird" is the Purple Finch first noticed in the spring in the apple trees among the blossoms.

Juncos are called "bluebirds" for their slate-blue feathers. In the winter, seen against the white snow, they are called "snowbirds."

To the "honeysuckle bird," the Ruby-throated Hummingbird, clings an old belief that they come north on the backs of ducks and geese. "They're so tiny they couldn't fly all the way north."

"Spiderbird" is the Black and White Warbler that probes its beak into the corners of window panes looking for spiders.

"Jay jack," "jay cat," "jay hawk," "carrion bird" are names for the Gray Jay, also known for its bold invasion of camps, as "camp thief," and "camp robber."

"St. John's Woodpecker" is the Black-backed Three-toed Woodpecker.

A "timberdoodle" is the American Woodcock. A "meadow hen" is the Common Snipe.

Both the Spruce and Ruffed Grouse are known as "partridge," and the Spruce Grouse as "silly bird" or "silly hen" because it can easily be caught by hand.

NAMES ASSOCIATED WITH SOUNDS

Some birds are known for their strident voices and for their rhythmic measures.

The Song Sparrow is known as "springbird" for its song, *sweet, sweet, sweet, spring, spring, spring.*

The far-away, flute-like evensong of the Hermit Thrush has given it the name "swamp robin."

For the booming sound the American Bittern makes when courting, "like someone hitting a stump with a wooden maul," it is called "pile driver," "rail splitter," "stake driver," "stump thumper," "stump pounder."

The Yellow-shafted Flicker for its hammering on trees and buildings, is called "yellow hammer."

SEA AND SHORE BIRDS

Sea and shore birds are also known for the sounds they make, for their habits, feathers and colours.

The "butternose," the Black Scoter, is named for the butter-yellow knob on the upper mandible of the male, and "patch poll," the Surf Scoter, for the patch of white on the male's head.

For their swirling, downward dive, Pied-billed Grebes are known as "hell-divers."

Spotted Sandpipers are "quiverwings" for the rapid quiver of their wings in flight.

The "seaweed bird" is the Ruddy Turnstone that searches for food in beds of seaweed rolled on the shore.

A "mud crack" is the Least Sandpiper that runs along the edge of the cracks in the mud flats; a "mud hen," a Wilson's Snipe.

The Great Blue Heron has long been known as a "crane." A lesser-known name is "pond loon," hence the expression, "as tall and straight as a pond loon."

Black-legged Kittiwakes that fly along the shores in the late fall, for their resemblance to gulls, are called "fall gulls." "Kaybreaks" are young loons.

"Parakeets" are the parrot-beaked Atlantic Puffins.

"Pineknots" are the tough little Dovekies, said to be as hard as a pineknot.

Arctic and Common Terns in their endless flight for tinkers, young mackerel, are called "mackerel gulls."

Willets have long been known as "Curlews," and also as "killy-willys" for their scolding call, *kill-will-willy*, to those who venture into their domain.

The flute-like notes of Piping Plovers have given them the name "pea blows." The whistling wings of the

Goldeneye, that of "whistlers," the peeps of Sandpipers that of "peepers."

Shearwaters have been nicknamed "hags," or "haglets."

Auks are known as "noddies."

Murres as "scribes." The Common Eiders are "sea ducks." Black Guillemots are "widgeons." Ospreys are called "seahawks." Purple Sandpipers are "winter oxeyes." Coots are "scouters."

Bobbing and diving and splashing water has given Coots the reputation of being silly birds, and the expressions "as silly as a coot," "a silly old coot," "as crazy as a coot."

A "pension" is a crippled bird or an old bird that lives apart from the flock. "It's like saying he's been pensioned off."

Double-crested cormorants are known as "shags," and their abundance has given Shag Harbour its name. Further along the shore, west of Shag Harbour, is a passage of water known as Cockerwit. In stories it was named for the call of the Oldsquaw duck, *cock-er-wit, cock-er-wit, cock-er-wit.*

How the Great Black-backed Gull was given the name "preacher" is an old story remembered in Shag Harbour. Before they became as numerous along the shores as they are today, as they did not follow the fish boats like the herring gulls, fishermen saw them only on Sundays. This was also the same and only day they saw the preacher. So, it is said, since they saw them only on the "preacher's day" they called them "preachers."

◆

Wild sea ducks are tough eating with prized recipes describing how to cook them. One, a recipe from Bon Portage, is for wild duck stew. Prepare your duck. Put it in a pot with vegetables. Cook until the vegetables are well done. Lift the lid and let the duck fly away. Eat what is left.

Another, the prized recipe of a Shelburne duck hunter, is for roast wild duck. Prepare your duck and stuff with a brick. Roast until the brick is tender. Throw away the duck. Eat the brick.

ANIMAL LORE

*I*n Shelburne County, where an old story says that cows have their noses filed to a point to crop the grass between the rocks, there are few farms, but there is animal lore and many old beliefs about animals, some only a memory; others still part of farm life.

COWS

Cattle, cows and oxen, are "critters," "creeturs." "In the old days father always killed a beef creetur every fall."

Singly or in pairs, a cow is a "bossie"; a single ox, a "dagen"; two oxen, a "yoke"; two horses, a "team." A bull is referred to as the "animal," "gentleman," or "agricultural ox." A "humble" cow is one without horns.

◆

Cows are called from the pasture with a mellow, "Co, co, co co bossie, co," or by name "Polly, Polly, Polly." A restless cow is soothed with a gentle, "So, so, bossie, so." A cow with a newborn calf has "just calv'd," "just come in," "just freshened," "is new flushed." Tansy tea was given to a cow when she "freshened," and hay tea and milk to her calf. Calves, when taken from their mothers at birth, were given skimmed milk mixed with their mother's new, thick milk, "beesling," with flax seeds added as the calf grew. In children's farm lore, a cow finds her calf under an old stump in the pasture.

In the barn, cows stood in a stall with a crib or manger, their heads held in a stanchel between two upright bars, the moveable bar held in place with a wooden peg. "Breechy" cows are unruly cows that hook the rails off fences, and sometimes go on a rampage. In the spring, when cows browse on a patch of "kilkid" (lambkill), they give bitter milk, called "kilkid milk." Cow dung is "cow patties," "cow paddies," "flops," "molasses pancakes," and is even referred to as "mountain daisies."

There are superstitions about cows. If a swallow is killed, a cow will give bloody milk. If a cow licks a window pane of her owner's house, there will be a death in the family.

OXEN

When there were many rocks to be dragged from rough land, a sure-footed ox served a farmer better than a horse. Oxen were first yoked with a "bow yoke" or "neck yoke"—a bent bow of wood slung beneath the neck of the ox and attached to a heavy wooden crosspiece across its neck. Iron rings beneath the crosspiece at either end held the shafts of sleds and dump carts. The "horn yoke" that replaced the older "bow yoke" is a wooden crosspiece shaped to rest on the head of an ox and lashed to the horns with a strap of leather. Bent over the centre of a "double horn yoke" are "hemmet irons," or bows with "hemmet chain" attached, to support the tongue of a cart thrust through the chain and secured to the yoke with a draw bolt.

There are many favourite names for a yoke of oxen. Bright, Spark, and Star for the "nigh" ox; Lion, Dime, and Brown for the "off" ox. When walking forward, the nigh ox is the nearest to the centre of the road. The off ox is nearest the side, and the driver, or teamster, always walks beside the nigh ox or directly in front of the two. Oxen are taught to "haw" (left) and "gee" (right), and to "back and haw," and to "back and gee." As "a comfort for an ox," one knit a net of twine to keep the flies off the animal.

Ox hauls, a proud tradition among those who train and own oxen, are still popular events. Yokes of oxen vie with each other to haul the greatest weight.

PIGS

A healthy pig has a curled tail, and a little pig with a curly tail is a good pig to buy. Around the use of the word "pig" a number of superstitions have grown: the word must never be used on board a vessel or on land for fear of ill luck in fishing and a disaster to fish boats. Even to talk about pigs will bring rain the next day.

When one kept a pig for the winter pork barrel, the bristles in the hide were removed with balsam fir in boiling water and wood ashes. The back of a sunburned pig was bathed with buttermilk. When a pig starts to raise old heck, there's a storm coming.

SHEEP

For sheep that roam the shores in flocks or mingle with other sheep in pastures, there are marks cut in their ears to identify their owners. These are registered as a "fork," a v-shaped cut in the edge of the ear; "crop-off," the top of the ear cropped off; a "ha'penny," a half-circle cut in the edge of the ear; and a "half-crop," when half the top of the ear is cropped off. One owner's marks for her sheep that roamed the Baccaro shores were:

Crop off the right, slit in the crop;
Fork off the left, and a ha'penny on top.

For another, her sheep's mark was two ha'pennies on the right ear.

When there were many sheep to provide wool to be spun into yarn for mitts and socks, and to be hooked into mats, Sheep Shearing Day every spring in Blanche was a day to remember.

HENS AND ROOSTERS

A hen is known as a "biddy." Some hens were given pet names: Bonny for a nice white hen; Dorothy Dingletail and Penelope were two hens that lived in Allendale. Some hens are more inclined to "set" than lay eggs. To persuade a hen back to her nest, a long red ribbon was tied to her tail. Running fast to escape the ribbon soon had her back on her nest laying eggs. Or a "broody" hen was hung on the clothesline in a "crocus bag." By sunset she was content to forget hatching chickens.

CATS AND DOGS

An all-black cat is bad luck. A small white spot, or even a few white hairs, breaks a cat's power for bad luck. To keep a cat from roaming, rub its paws with butter. The cat will lick its paws, like the butter and stay home. Cats are said to have nine lives and "there are more ways to kill a cat than choking it with butter." When cats are frisky, a storm is brewing, it will rain the day after a cat washes behind its ears, and whichever way a cat's tail points when asleep the wind will blow the next day.

When dogs "bay at the moon" there has been a death in the community; and in times of an approaching crisis dogs howling in the night foretell a disaster.

Dogs are believed to be psychic. In Sandy Point, there was a dog so devoted to his mistress that every morning when she opened her bedroom door and walked into the living room to sit in the bay window, the dog walked beside her and slept at her feet on the braided rug. When she died, the dog grieved her passing. One day when the rest of the family were sitting together in the living room, the dog suddenly woke up and, wagging his tail, walked to the old woman's door, and then, as in days past when he walked beside her, he walked across the living room to her chair, still in its old place beside the window, and with a happy whimper of contentment went to sleep on the braided mat.

In Shelburne there was a dog whose spirit lived on after her death. When Dawna was born, her fur was the colour of a golden dawn. She lived a long life. When she died, those she had loved, and those who had loved her, buried her in a wooded lot among tall spruce trees. On the way home, as they drove along the road, they heard the panting sound of Dawna running behind the car, and then came the strange odour that had been in her fur when she died. Then she was "in the car," in the back seat, where she always sat watching the road ahead. Soon the scent and the sound faded, and those who had loved her marvelled that her dog spirit came to them, and is a cherished memory.

HOME REMEDIES FOR DOMESTIC ANIMALS

For some of the illnesses suffered by animals there were home remedies and when they failed, the "horse doctor" was called in to administer cures he might know. For a sick cow, a local "horse doctor" in Port La Tour arrived with a bundle of herbs, bark, and roots. He ordered hemlock to be steeped and placed hot on the cow's back, covered and bound in place with crocus bags. Another remedy for a sick cow was smoke from a fire kindled with old shoes, rope, and tar which made her cough "and started her off on the road back to good health."

Rope burns, caused by a rope chafing the leg or back of a cow or horse, were bathed with epsom salts, and kept moist with a salve made from lard and sulphur. When a cow or ox knocked off a horn, the stub was painted with tar and wrapped with a cloth.

For a calf with "scours" (diarrhoea), the remedy given was steeped fall dandelions; for a horse, it was an ounce of catechu in water.

In Shelburne, a half-and-half mixture of steeped tansy and beef pickle, with a piece of saltpetre, the size of a thumbnail, and turpentine, was used to bathe swellings and sores on horses. A dog's sore head was bathed with salt water.

For colic in calves, when their sides were swollen stiff from eating new grass, a sharp knife was driven several times into the calf's belly to release the pressure.

In Sandy Point a lamb suffered a similar painful swelling of the stomach from eating the new leaves of kilkid. Melted pork lard and molasses was poured down the lamb's throat to force the leaves to be disgorged.

For a droopy hen, a very good cure was to put her in a box with a warm board beneath her feet.

INSECTS AND SNAKES

♦ INSECTS ♦

There are superstitions, old beliefs, and rhymes about insects.

RHYMES

To a ladybug held in the hands is chanted:

Ladybug, ladybug,
Fly away home,
Your house is on fire,
Your children will burn.

A captive grasshopper is told:

Grasshopper, Grasshopper.
Give us some molasses.
If you don't I'll chop off your head.

Of bees, it is said:

A swarm of bees in May,
Is worth a load of hay.
A swarm of bees in June,

Is worth a silver spoon.
A swarm of bees in July,
Is not worth a fly.

WEATHER

Insects know well in advance what the weather will be in the depths of winter: when caterpillars have thick coats of fur in the fall, there will be a long, cold, winter; when hornets build their nests high in the bushes, the winter will be heavy with snow; nests built close to the ground, foretell a mild winter and little snow. Before a spring rain, if there are many ants scurrying over the ground, there will be a dry, hot summer.

SUPERSTITIONS

To crush a spider is bad luck, and poor health and misfortune will follow the one who crushed it. Besides, to kill a spider will bring a heavy downpour of rain. If a spider gets in a house it must be gathered gently in a soft cloth and returned outdoors.

"Devil's darning-needles" are big, black, overgrown dragonflies that will sew your eyelids together. Fireflies that sparkle over misty meadows in July are lightning bugs. "If it weren't for 'lightning bugs' how could the mosquitoes get around in the dark."

"Fallflies" look like bumble bees and drone around the windows in the fall of the year. The same fallflies are known as "yarnflies" for their humming drone like the humming of a spinning wheel.

Inchworms are foreboding. If one inches its way unforeseen from your toes to your head you will die, for it has measured you for your coffin.

◆ SNAKE LORE ◆

In old beliefs, snakes are evil and should be killed. Kill the first snake to emerge in the spring, and all one's enemies will be overcome. When killed, snakes twitch their tails until sundown. A dead snake lying belly-up will bring a downpour of rain; flipped over on its belly, back up, the sun will shine.

When young snakes are in danger, their mother swallows her babies. She opens her mouth wide and they crawl in one by one. When the danger has passed, she opens her mouth and they emerge safely.

A snake is made from a long hair from a horse's tail, from which, when spread on the surface of green, stagnant water will start to twitch and then a snake will form and crawl from the water. Two boys in Coffinscroft pulled a long hair from the tail of a horse and laid it on stagnant water. They watched for days as the hair was wrapped in green algae and the snake was getting ready to leave. Then, when they were not there, the snake got away.

FISH AND AMPHIBIANS

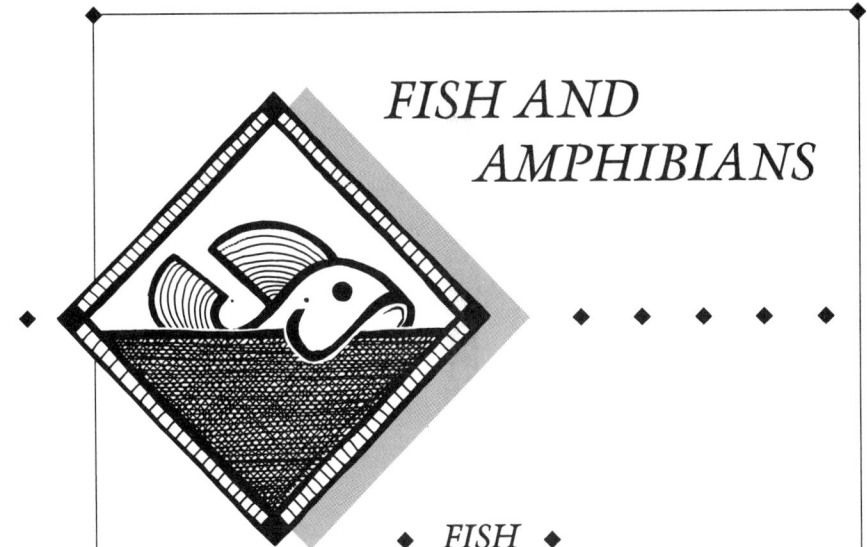

♦ FISH ♦

In the shallow pools left by the receding tide are minnows and sticklebacks caught by children in scoop nets they have woven from bulrushes. Minnows are known as "gudgeons" in Barrington, as "killyfish" in Shelburne, as "minneyfish" in Villagedale. Eels are "squirmers", "because they keep on squirming after they are dead, just like dead snakes twitch their tails until sundown."

Sea urchins are called "sea eggs"; hermit crabs that live in old discarded cockle shells are called "scrubblejacks." Smelt that come into sheltered coves in early winter and are caught through holes cut in the ice are known as "frost fish." "Drummers" are red-bellied sculpins that inflate when their red bellies are tickled, and float like puffy balloons when tossed back in the water. They are called "scoggies" on Cape Island, where one fisherman wrote the following poem in the 1940s:

Puff-bellied scoggy, can you swim?
Yes, by golly, when the tide comes in.

Puff-bellied scoggy, can you float?
Yes, by golly, when the tide goes out.

Fishermen have given names to many species of sea creatures. Dolphins are called "pilot fish" because they usually come in twos, one each side of the bow, like pilots guiding a boat to a safe harbour; porpoises are called "puffins" because they give three blows before they go underwater. "Tommy cod" are young codfish; "sand dab" is a flounder; "bloaters" are large herring. Catfish, the Atlantic wolf fish, reputed to have a "hide as tough as a blacksmith's apron," and renamed "monkfish," is sold as "monktail." An old name on Cape Island for a lobster is "soroggan."

"Kiacks" swarm into the rivers in early spring and are caught in long-handled dip nets as they struggle upstream to their spawning grounds. In a smoke house, over smudge fires of bark and chips, they are smoked a golden brown, with tussocks of ferns sometimes added to the fire for a special flavour. Kiack, a species of herring known to the Acadians as "gaspereau," is perhaps a word with Micmac origins, or as some suggest, they were named for their resemblance to kayaks. Kiack roes were an old home remedy for worms.

"Tinkers," "tholepins," and "spikes" are young fish; tinker mackerel are also known as "shiners" for their shimmering silver as they swim in schools near the surface of the water. Slender, young kiacks are "fingerlings." Small lobsters are also known as tinkers, and an undersized lobster is a "midget," a "jinx." A shelled cooked lobster is referred to as "pink fish." "Smellers" are the long feelers on the head of lobsters and squid; "fish peas" are fish roes. A lobster is "he," and to one lobsterman, "He'em all good to eat."

In Birchtown, there is a version of the old tale of why haddock have black lines scratched in their sides. In the story, the devil was standing in water when a fish came swimming by. He grabbed it, shouting, "Hey, Dick. I got ya." The fish flipped out of the devil's claws and was gone, but it still bears black claw marks to this day.

◆ AMPHIBIANS ◆

"Pink winks" are spring peepers. They say *pink-wink, pink, pe-weep*. In the same pond with the pink winks, are clusters of frogs' and toads' eggs and swirling "pollywogs" (tadpoles) that have just hatched from the clusters of eggs. In the spring nights are heard their voices:

The pink wink says,
Pee weep, pee weep.
Cold feet
Can't sleep.

The Big frog says,
Brum, brum.
Go to sleep.
And hush your tongue

◆

There was an Irishman who listened to pink winks and frogs when he came to the Barrington River and wanted to cross the river to the other side. He hesitated, uncertain of the depth of the water. A voice piped, "Knee deep. Knee deep." He stepped into the water and a gruff voice warned, "Better-go-round. Better-go-round."

PLANTS, TREES AND LICHENS

◆ PLANTS ◆

For many plants, local names have supplanted the common, and more widely-used names. In Sable River, "buca" is an old name for bearberry that grows in abundance on dry barren land. Growing alongside it is "fox's bedding" (crowberry) also known as "snakes' eyes" for its tiny black berries like the black eyes of a snake. With buca and fox's bedding grows "ginger plums" (checkerberries or wintergreen), known as "teaberry" in Lower Ohio and as "winterberry" for their bright-red berries that still have a sharp flavour when lifted out of the snow. Creeping snowberry, for the flavour of its snow-white fruit is known as "wineberry"; and partridgeberry is "eyeberry," "snakeberry," "hog plum," and "hogberry."

Fear of snakes lurking in long grass where wild blue iris (blue flag) grows has given it the name "snake flag." From their seedpods, small boats can be carved, which sail with a toothpick mast and a paper sail; and from the leaves, sail boats are fashioned by bending the sharp tip into a slit cut in the rib of the leaf. Placed on the surface of the water, they sail away in the wind.

Also mindful of snakes, lurking beneath the low branches of ground juniper it is called "snakepatch" in Villagedale and Coffinscroft.

On bogs and savannahs grow "bakeapple," "baked apple" (cloudberry), the tart flavour of its amber berries suggestive of baked crabapples. In earlier times, it was called "bec' apples," according to sources in Barrington and Baccaro. In Green Harbour bakeapples are called "wild pears."

In May, the wide savannahs are white with "cotton top," "bog cotton," "wild cotton"; and in clumps of spoon-like leaves grow pitcherplants, called "Indian pitchers," "Indian pipes," "Indian spoons." Edging the same savannahs are cat-tails, "pussy-tails," and "puss-tails."

Used by midwives in Shag Harbour as a diuretic following childbirth, the dandelion, was given the name "pissabed." Ground ivy, with leaves like the soft foot-pads of a cat is "cat's paw." Seaside plantain was known in Barrington as "goose tongue," until a minister gathered it as a green and it was renamed "minister's grass" and "minister's green." Jimson-weed, grown for its leaves to be dried and smoked as a relief from asthma, was called "Angel's triumph."

"Knee-high buckwheat," "knee-high Washington," "rambling sailors" are local names for Japanese knotweed, a fairly recent import in the Lockeport and Shelburne areas, where it grows in great bamboo-like stalks. "Johnny juniper," "jolly jumper," "johnny jump-up," "ladies delight" are names for the tiny pansy, viola tricolour. In Lower Ohio, St. John's wort is called "royal George."

"Smilin' Cina" is an old Barrington name for the pretty, wild lily-of-the-valley. In Green Harbour it is "toothbrush."

PLANTS FROM OTHER LANDS

The story of how Scotch broom came to "New Scotland" has many versions. In one story of the broom, it was brought to the Jordan-Shelburne area by Lauchlan McPherson, grandfather of the renowned builder of clipper ships, Donald McKay. In other stories it was brought by someone lonely for the broom, or it came in straw bed-ticks from Scotland.

In an old story from East Jordan, Scotch heather that blooms beside the roadway came from the old homeland as seeds embedded in the mud clinging to a Scotsman's boots.

May apple, nicknamed "mammy-apples," was brought to Shelburne from the United States. They are remembered as growing first in a garden, near the north end of Mowat Street, Shelburne. The old York and Lancaster rose, whose pink and white petals are a symbol of the War of the Roses, was brought to Shelburne, according to local tradition, by two families, and was known as "Purdy Rose," or "Bruce Rose," and in recent years as "Loyalist Rose."

PLANT LORE

From years of watching the flow of the seasons, including the influence of the moon, the lore for planting crops and cutting trees has been gathered.

It is bad luck to plant a garden on any day except on the rising of the new moon. With the new moon, life flows upward; with the growing moon, the sap glides through the tree. If the bark is to be removed from a hemlock, cut it on the growing moon when the sap lies beneath the bark. For dry firewood of maple or birch, cut the trees on the dark of the moon in August. To rid the land of unwanted alders, pull them up by the root before the full of the moon in July or August.

Nature is mindful of her own. When there are many berries on the rowan trees, on the vines of partridge berry, and on Canada holly, and when there are many "rose buds," wild rose hips, there will be a hard, long winter with deep snow, for Mother Nature knows how the seasons will roll and provides an abundance of berries and seeds for the birds, and cones on the tall spruce trees for the squirrels.

In children's lore, a lady dressed in gold sits within the petals of a blue violet bathing her feet in nectar. Where a lone lady's slipper is found, there once walked an Indian princess who lost one of her pretty mocassins. A purple-red floret in the centre of Queen Anne's lace is said to be the blood of Queen Anne, where she pricked her busy fingers. To play King Midas' game, a branch of alder leaves is held in golden-amber brook water to turn the leaves to gold.

SUPERSTITIONS

Superstitions about flowers and plants are part of local lore. A houseplant that grows with great vigour "is growing on someone," and must be destroyed. A few, fearful of the colour green, will not allow a houseplant in their houses.

One must never say thank you for the gift of a plant

for "plants don't like to be given away." A stolen plant grows best, especially one that has survived the years beside an old abandoned homestead. A flower growing on a grave must never be picked or its roots plucked from the earth.

Some people will not pick and carry wildflowers into a house for fear of bad luck, as a little girl in Shelburne discovered when she picked a good luck four-leaf clover and took it to her grandfather. He was a gentle old man, but he pushed her aside and ordered her to leave, with the stern command never to enter his house again with a four-leaf clover.

There is an old belief that when violets bloom late in the fall, an epidemic will spread through a community.

◆ TREES AND SHRUBS ◆

Shrubs and trees have been given significant names. "Pinks" is the name given to rhodora for its magenta-pink flowers that cover the land with a pink haze, even before its leaves unfold. Sheep laurel is called "kilkid" because its virulent green leaves kill sheep and their lambs. Witherod has many names: "withewood," "withe," "sheepberries," for its clusters of blueberries, "sheep tassels," "Indian arrows," and "broom" for the barn brooms that were made from its slender branches. Named for its uses, *Ilex glabra* is called "inkberry" and "dyeberry." "Partridge berry bush," in Sandy Point, is a name for black alder for its red berries like those on partridgeberry vines. Black alder is also known as "Canada holy" for its red berries.

An old dark-skinned birch is a "monkey birch." Poplar is "popple," or "silver popple." Dogwood (mountain ash) is "prickle ash," "prickly ash," and "rowan," and is known as the "witch's tree," because its wood is used by fishermen to make rollers on boats, "to keep the witches away." Hackmatack, the tamarack or larch provided the natural "grown knees," or "ship's knees" used as ribs in the construction of boats and dories, and made very good hockey sticks.

"Cat spruce" is a slender spruce with sharp pointed needles that give off an unpleasant odour when its branches are broken. "Scrub spruce," stunted cat spruce, that grows on wind-beaten shores and crouches on the barrens, its growth crippled by the wind. On a wind-swept shore, it leans away from the wind, making thick canopies of branches close to the ground that provide shelter for sheep.

"Spills," or "tree bristles," are the slender needle-like, sharp-tipped leaves of the conifers. In Lower Ohio, pine spills are "quills" and are used when they fall to the ground as insulation to bank a house against the cold drafts of winter.

The new growth on the tips of the branches of fir and spruce trees, called "buds," when stripped of their spills, are as tasty as a stick of candy, as are "tags," alder catkins, when their rough covering is rubbed from the "string," the core of the catkin. For children, sap-filled "blisters" in the bark of the balsam fir are a source of fairy-colours; when the sap is swished across a pool of water, it spreads like rainbows over the water. "Cramp knots" squeezed in the hands to ease aching muscles, are shaped from "humps" and tree knots.

◆ LICHENS, FERNS, CLUBMOSSES AND FUNGI ◆

Lichens and clubmosses, ferns and fungi have attracted names descriptive of their appearance. "Scabs" and "barnacles" are names given to the rough grey clusters of lichen that cover rocks and the bark of old trees. "Cockles" or "crockers" are the brittle leaves of lichen on granite boulders, like the shells of sea cockles. "Billy-run-away," as its name suggests, is a club moss that runs beneath the ground cover.

Through the matted hummocks of dried fronds and root stocks, ferns thrust their rolled "fiddleheads." An edible nut-like kernel in the centre of a clump of cinnamon fern has been given many names by children who pull up the unfolding fiddleheads for the "meat," "banana," "nigger toes," "nigger meat," or "monkey meat."

"Bear biscuit" or "bear bread" grows like shelves on trees. It was cut from the bark and a design etched in the biscuit, then touched up with colour, making an attractive curio on a whatnot. "Daddy oakum," "old man's beard," or "old man's whiskers" (*usnea barbata*), hangs in long festoons on old trees in sheltered woodland, and along windy shores clings close to the bark of broken branches. "Witch's broom" stands tall on branches of spruce trees, a tiny replica of the tree that gives them a sheltered site to grow.

THE LORE OF CHILDREN

Although many adults have forgotten or have pushed aside old beliefs and well-seasoned customs, games and rhymes that are the lore of children have withstood the test of time. The delight and happiness in playing and the reciting of counting-out rhymes, skipping songs, and tongue twisters never ends for children.

♦ COUNTING-OUT RHYMES ♦

There are many counting-out rhymes to determine who will be "it." They express delight in the bright, lively words and rhythm.

An old rhyme which was popular in the Shelburne school yard in the 1880s and 1890s was,

Aina, maina, mona, mike,
Barcelona, bona, strike;
Here, where, flounce Jack,
Ballaco, wallaco, we, woe, whack.

This rhyme is of particular interest in the way it may have been introduced into Shelburne County. A similar rhyme was collected in New York City in 1815, where, forty years earlier, it would have been learned by children who came with their Loyalist parents to Shelburne in 1783. This lively rhyme soon drifted to other children, perhaps introduced to the early New England settlements along the shores when their parents left Shelburne and found new homes among the old settlers. As with all rhymes that delight children, it was changed, a word here, a word there—and in Shag Harbour in the 1880s the children said,

Eenie, meenie, mynee, moe,
Passa, lona, bona, strae;
Air, ware, flounce, flack,
Ellaka, wellaka, wee, woe, why, wack.

In Lower Ohio in the same decade, the children were saying,

Mica, mona, mina, mike,
Passa, lona, bona, strike;
Air, where, frown, hack,
Hareico, wareico, wee, woe, whack.

Across the Roseway River, in Welshtown, the children knew still another variant of the old rhyme, they said,

Eena, mena, mina, mike,
Barcelona, bona, strike;
Care, ware, frow,
Hallico, wallico, we, woe, whack.

Among the older rhymes familiar to children in Shelburne in the early 1900s were:

Eena, mena, dipper, deena,
Hatcha, patcha, dominatcha;

High, pan, tippety, toss,
Out she goes.

Ivory, ovory, ickary Ann,
Filsery, folsery, Nicholas John;
Quivary, quovary, Irish man,
Stinklum, stonklum, buck—
You're out.

In the 1960s, a little boy was saying:

Enty, menty, tibbety, fig,
Adelia, delia, domenig,
Icha, bitcha, domanicha.
Om, bom, tusk,
Ellika, bellika, boo. Out goes Y-O-U.

A rhyme popular in Sable River was,

Ibbity, bibbity, sibbity, sab,
Ibbity, bibbity, canal boat,
Dictionary down the ferry,
Out goes Y-O-U.

Another popular rhyme in Sable River was,

Inkity, minkity, tethery tuss,
Drinking milk is good for us.
Inkity, minkity, tethery toe,
We drink milk wherever we go.

Among the counting-out rhymes enjoyed by the children at the Hawk, were:

My father had an old horseshoe
How many nails did he put through.
(The counting goes on to the number named.)

They enjoyed the snappy little rhyme:

By the hokey, by the pokey,
By the pinky, by the panky,
How do you do?
Very well, I thank ye.

Longer counting rhymes were recited at the Hawk with as much glee as their short rhymes, as this one about grandfather's cat:

Grandfather's cat wouldn't do any harm,
She caught all the rats and mice in grandfather's barn.
Grandfather had some wheat and rye.
He put it out in the barn to dry;
Out came the mice to have some fun.
Up jumped the pussy cat, and made them all run.

The children at the Hawk also loved counting-out rhymes, with jumping and dancing as they counted:

I love to jump,
I love to shout,
Y-O-U are out.

I love to dance,
I love to shout,
Y-O-U are out.

The most widely known of all counting-out rhymes was also the best known rhyme in Shelburne County:

Eeny, meeny, miny, mo,
Catch a nigger by the toe;
If he hollers let him go,
Eeny, meeny miny mo.

When this rhyme was recited in Barrington schoolyards in the early 1900s, the racist connotation was not an issue. In recent times, "nigger" has been replaced by "tiger."

In Sable River the children added:

Hot potatoes on his chin,
Nuff to make the devil grin.

In Shelburne the children knew another old rhyme that is no longer acceptable.

Nigger, nigger, never die,
Black face and shiny eyes;
Thick lips and flat nose,
And on the head the wool grows.

There were many snappy short rhymes:

Ittle, ottle, black bottle,
Ittle, ottle blue bottle
Ittle ottle, out.

Ink, mink, who stinks
Like any old mink
O-U-T spells out and out you must go.
and:
Pink, wink, you stink.

Counting out rhymes with numbers were popular in Lockeport and Shelburne:

1, 2, 3, 4, 5,
I caught a fish alive;
6, 7, 8, 9, 10,
I let him go again.

1, 2, 3, 4, 5, 6, 7,
All good children go to heaven,
One goes up and one goes down,
One goes way back and sits down.

1 potato, 2 potatoes, 3 potatoes, 4,
5 potatoes, 6 potatoes, 7 potatoes, lore,
8 potatoes, 9 potatoes, 10 potatoes, more,
Out you go.

Many of these thymes are still heard today. A favourite in the Shelburne schoolyard is,

Engine, engine, number nine,
Going down the Chicago line;
If the train went off the track,
Do you want your money back?

If the answer is "yes," the count continues, "Y-E-S out goes Y-O-U." If "no," the count is "N-O out goes Y-O-U."

From the Shelburne schoolyard came this rhyme:

Razza, pazza, pizza pie,
Ruddle, puddle pie.
You've a cinder in your eye.
That's why you are it.

In Welshtown the children know a relatively new rhyme:

Inky, pinky, ponky,
Daddy bought a donkey.
Donkey died, Daddy cried,
Inky, pinky, ponky.

A rhyme for counting-out long enjoyed by the children of Coffinscroft and Woods Harbour was,

Inty, minty, diddle-dee-fee,
Diamond, iamond, omond, ee,
Oochy, boochy, diamond oochy,
Hong Kong cuff,
Ellica, bellica, boo,
Out goes Y-O-U.

◆ SKIPPING RHYMES ◆

Like counting-out rhymes, skipping rhymes have long histories, and words have been changed to suit the times, but the rhythm is universal. In the Ragged Islands schoolyard, where there are other children from the nearby communities of Sable River, Little Harbour, Osborne Harbour and Squirrel Valley, the rules for skipping and swinging the skip-rope are in the rhymes. To begin, there are "first end" and "second end," a child to swing each end of the rope. To swing and jump the rope:

Slow go. (jump the rope while it is being swung slowly)
Run through. (run through while the rope is being swung)
One foot. (jump on one foot three times)
Touch the ground. (touch the ground three times)
Jolly o' pepper. (jump while the rope is swung very fast)

For a birthday rhyme, they skip:

Apples, oranges, peaches, plums,
Jump right out when your birthday comes:
January, February, March, April, May,
June, July, August, September,

October, November, December.
One, two, three, four ...

The counting at the end of many of the rhymes is jumped to the fast speed of "pepper."

Other favourite rhymes in the Ragged Islands schoolyard are as follows:

Dutch girl, Dutch girl,
Do the split—split—split.
Dutch girl, Dutch girl,
Give a high kick—kick—kick.
Dutch girl, Dutch girl,
Turn around—'round—'round.
Dutch girl, Dutch girl,
Touch the ground—ground—ground.
Dutch girl, Dutch girl,
Get out of town—town—town—town.

Unka, onka, neeka,
Five, six, seven, eight.
I met my boyfriend (girlfriend) at the candy store.
He bought me candy,
He bought me cake,
He brought me home with a belly ache.
Mama ... Mama ... I'm so sick,
Call the doctor quick, quick, quick.
Doctor ... Doctor ... will I die?
Not unless you count to five.
One ... two ... three ... four ... five,
I'm alive!

Cinderella, dressed in yellow,
She went upstairs to kiss a fellow,
She made a mistake and kissed a snake

How many doctors does it take,
One ... two ... three ... etc.
(Count while the rope is being swung normally, or using "pepper.")

Peel a banana upside down,
Peel an orange round and round,
If you reach to twenty-four,
You may have your turn once more.
One ... two ... three ...

I had a little car in 1957
I took it on a trip around the cor ... ner.
(the skipper goes around the rope swingers)
And then slammed on the brakes.
But my brakes wouldn't work,
The police caught me and put me in jail.
How many ginger ales did I drink.
One ... two ... three ...

A number of the skipping rhymes in the Ragged Islands schoolyard are also familiar to the children in Shelburne where "Peel a Banana" and "I bought a Car" are favourites. Two other rhymes skipped in Shelburne are,

I had a little brother,
and his name was Tiny Tim.
I put him in the bathtub,
To teach him how to swim.
He drank up all the water,
And he ate up all the soap.
It made him feel very ill,
With bubbles in his throat.

Mabel, Mabel, set the table,
Don't forget the salt, mustard, vinegar, pepper
(Here the rope is swung very fast to make the skipper miss the rope.)

◆ RHYMES, VERSES, AND TONGUE TWISTERS ◆

Many of the rhymes and verses are told by mothers and grandmothers to their children and grandchildren, as the following from Shag Harbour:

Oh, holy father, I've come to confess.
Well, daughter Jane, I'm ready to bless.
Oh, holy father, our old cat stole a fish.
Well, daughter Jane, that's nothing amiss.
Oh, holy father, I killed the old cat.
Well, daughter Jane, you must suffer for that.
Oh, holy father, what must I do?
Well, daughter Jane, you kiss me and I'll kiss you.

Another old verse is remembered as grandmother's ditty.

A man of words and not of deeds,
Is like a garden full of weeds,
And when the weeds begin to grow,
Is like a garden full of snow.
And when the snow begins to melt,
Is like a garden full of hemp,
And when the hemp begins to fly,
Is like an eagle in the sky.
And when the sky begins to roar,

Is like a lion at the door,
And when the door begins to crack,
It's like a stick across your back,
And when your back begins to fail,
It's like a ship under sail.
And when the ship begins to sink,
It's like a bottle full of ink,
And when the ink begins to write,
It's like an old man with his pipe!

A lively rhyme enjoyed by a little boy in Shelburne is "Hoomp-me-shoomp-me-sharny."

As I went up the hoomp-me-shoomp,
The hoomp-me-shoomp-me-sharny,
I met a great big hoomp-me-shoomp,
Eating my cabarney.
If I had my hoomp-me-shoomp,
My hoomp-me-shoomp-me-sharny,
I would have shot that hoomp-me-shoomp,
For eating my cabarney.

The same little boy in Shelburne enjoyed a rhyme his father sang and taught him.

Did you ever see the devil
  with a wood and iron shovel,
Diggin' tatters by the bushel
  with his long coat on.

When the tatters got so big
  the devil couldn't dig
He just strutted round the garden
  with his long coat on.

Two rhymes were taught to a little girl in Shelburne by the old lady "who lives in the lane."

Robert and Bobbit and big-bellied Ben,
Could eat more meat than four score men.
Could eat a cow and a calf,
An ox and a half,
A church and a steeple,
And all the good people,
And then complained that his belly wasn't full.

Over the river and over the sea,
Over the river to Charley,
Charley loves good cake and wine,
Charley loves good brandy,
Charley loves to kiss the girls,
As sweet as sugar candy.

There are other rhymes known in Shelburne and Barrington:

A fly and a flea got caught in a flue,
And then they wondered what they should do.
Said the fly, "Let us flea." Said the flea, "Let us fly."
So they fled through a flaw in the flue.

One, two, three,
Mamma caught a flea,
Flea died, and mamma cried,
Oh, dear me.

In Welshtown, the children have a rhyme about the colour of eyes.

Blue-eyed beauty,
Do your mother's duty,

Black-eyed pick a pie,
Turn around and tell a lie.

A little girl in North East Harbour learned and remembered this rhyme about snuff:

Put your diabolical fingers in my pathetic snuff box,
And take a sniff of my extravagancy.
It will incinerate your nostrils,
And make your head feel quite salubrious.

It was fun to chant a rhythm that fits the words:

Matthew, Mark, Luke and John,
Take a stick and walk along.

Preface was a very special word in school books, for the letters fitted a rhyme:

Preface
Peter Ross eats fish, alligators catch eels.
then backward:
Eels catch Alligators, Freeman (fish) eats raw potatoes.

Two tongue-twisters were mastered by the children at the Hawk:

Susan shineth shoes and socks,
Socks and shoes shineth Susan;
She ceaseth shining shoes and socks,
For socks and shoes shock Susan.

Peter Piper picked a peck of pickled peppers,
A peck of pickled peppers Peter Piper picked;
If Peter Piper picked a peck of pickled peppers,
Where's the peck of pickled peppers Peter Piper picked.

Counting daisies and fingers and playing rhyming action games, like knock-knock, are part of growing up.

Knock, knock, at the door.
Who's there?
An old grenadier.
What do you want?
A bottle of beer.
Where's your money?
Oh, I forgot.
Get along home, you old drunken sot!

Counting daisy petals is fun, though not always truthful. In Welshtown, as they pull the petals from a daisy, the children say,

One I love, two he loves, three I love I say,
Four I love with all my heart, five I cast away.
Six he loves, seven she loves, eight both love,
Nine he comes, ten he tarries,
Eleven he courts, twelve he marries.

Daisies were also asked to predict the profession of a girl's future husband:

Rich man, poor man, beggar man, thief; doctor, lawyer, merchant, chief.

To count fingers, an old man in Barrington Passage taught his little granddaughters,

Thumb man gate, (thumb)
Lick pot sweet, (index finger)
Long man ling, (middle finger)
Little man king, (fourth finger)
Little Jack a-darling, (little finger)

This little pig went to market (thumb)
This little pig stayed home (index finger)
This little pig had roast beef (third finger)
This little pig had none (fourth finger)
This little pig said, "Wee, wee," all the way home (little finger)

This "little pig" finger rhyme, is known in Clarks Harbour:

First little pig says, "Let's go up to grandfather's farm."
This little pig says, "What for?"
This little pig says, "Steal meat."
This little pig says, "I'll tell."
This little pig says, "Wee, wee, I can't get over the big barn door."

Another finger rhyme from Clarks Harbour goes:

"Little pea, little pea, where are you going?" (little finger)
     "I'm going with my dear sister Tillie Lou."
     "Tillie Lou, Tillie Lou, pray where are you going?"(fourth finger)
     "I'm going with my next bigger sister, Lou Whistle."
     "Lou Whistle, Lou Whistle, pray where are you going?"(third finger)
     "I'm going with my dear sister Bess Throstle."
     "Bess Throstle, Bess Throstle, pray where are you going?" (index finger)
     "I'm going with big brother Tommy Bumble."(thumb)
     "Little folks, little folks, where are you all going?"
     "We're up, we're going down, we're going in,
     We're going out, we're going, we're going,
     We're going, we're going right under the dimple in Baby's own chin."

In Shelburne, fingers are known as: little man (little finger), ring man (third finger), long man (second finger), fore man (index finger)

◆ FABLES ◆

THE OLD WOMAN WHO LIVED IN A VINEGAR BOTTLE

The story of the old woman who lived in a vinegar bottle was told many times over by a woman in Clarks Harbour to her two little daughters, that they should never forget what happens to the greedy.

Once upon a time there was an old woman who lived in a vinegar bottle. One day, when she was sweeping the floor, she found a silver penny and off she went to market to see what she could buy. As she went along, she met a woman with pretty little fish for sale.

"I'll give you one of these fish, missus," said the woman, "for your silver penny."

"Very well," said the old woman. "Here's my penny, and I'll have this fish."

The fisherwoman dropped the fish in the basket, and the old lady started off home to cook her fish for supper. As she went along, the fish lifted its head and pleaded in a gentle voice, "Please put me in the water. Please put me in the water." The old woman was so astonished she went to a stream close by and dropped the fish in the water. No sooner had she done so than the water began to bubble, bubble, bubble, and a pretty fairy stood before her.

"I am the little fish you put in the water," said the fairy. Ask of me anything you like, and I will give it to you."

The old woman was so astonished, she could harldy speak. Then she said, "Please, good fairy, give me a house, for I have only a vinegar bottle to live in."

"Very well," said the fairy. "Go home and you will find a house." And the fairy disappeared beneath the sparkling water.

The old woman hurried home as fast as her old legs could carry her, and there, sure enough, instead of a vinegar bottle, was a dear house, with a kitchen and a parlour downstairs, and two bedrooms upstairs. Oh! how happy she was! She moved the furniture from the vinegar bottle around in her rooms and sat down to admire her home.

Then she began to notice the furniture was very shabby, and how little she had, for how much furniture can one have in a vinegar bottle! "Perhaps," she thought, "the fairy will give me some furniture." Off she started for the stream and called in a soft voice, "Fairy! Fairy!" The water began to bubble, bubble, bubble, and the fairy stood before her.

"What do you want, my good woman?" asked the fairy.

"Why ma'am, if you please, will you give me some furniture to go in the house you have been so good to give me."

"Go home, and you will find some," said the fairy as she sank beneath the water.

The old woman trudged home, and it was all true. Such beautiful furniture in her dear house. For days she was happy, and then she began to wish for something more, and off she went to the stream, and called in a loud voice, "Fairy! Fairy!" The water began to bubble, bubble, bubble, and the fairy stood before her.

"Well, my good woman, what is it now that you want?"

"Well, ma'am, if you please," answered the old woman, "you have been so kind to give me the house and furniture, but I can't take care of it for I am so old. Will you be so good as to give me a maid to help me."

"Very well," said the fairy. "Go home, and you will find a little maid to help you."

The old woman went home and there was a little maid, broom in hand, busily sweeping the floors of her house. The old woman was happy for a week, content with what she had. Then she began to wish for something more, and again she went to the stream. In a loud and commanding voice she called, "Fairy! Fairy!" The water began to bubble, bubble, bubble and the fairy stood before her. "Well, old woman," demanded the fairy. "What do you want today?"

The old woman replied, "Why, ma'am you have been so very good to me, and have given me a house and furniture, and a little maid. Now, if you please, give me a cart and a horse to take me to market."

"Go home," said the fairy, "and you will find them. But beware of discontent!"

The old woman was rather frightened by the fairy's stern warning. She went home slowly and thought that now she would be content with what she had for, when she arrived home, there was a covered cart and a brown horse to draw it. She and her little maid drove off to market, and all her neighbours called her "the fortunate old lady."

But soon she was not content with what she had, and, forgetting the fairy's stern warning, she again went to the edge of the stream. "Fairy! Fairy!" she called. The water began to bubble, bubble, bubble, and again the fairy stood before her and demanded sternly, "My good woman what can you possibly want from me today?"

The old woman was frightened, but she said to the fairy, "Why, if you please, good fairy, you have been so very kind to me, but I really do not think I ought to ride about just like the women in the neighbourhood in a covered cart. So, if you please, will you give me a coach and four."

"What," exclaimed the fairy angrily. "What more will you ask for! Go home to your vinegar bottle." And down she sank beneath the water, never to rise again when the old woman called, "Fairy! Fairy!"

The old woman went home trembling. When she got there, there was only her old vinegar bottle with its ladder to get in and to get out. And there she lived alone all the rest of her days.

THE STORY OF THE GOLDEN ARM

In Lockeport the children had a story they liked to re-tell again and again.

There was once a man who lost one arm. He was a very rich man and had a golden arm made, instead of a wooden one, to replace his lost arm. When he died, he was buried with his golden arm. For many years he lay buried in his grave. Then, a couple of men remembered the golden arm and decided to dig him up and steal his golden arm. They were careful to push all the gravel back in the grave, but a policeman walking through the cemetery noticed some mud and loose gravel in the grass. He knew the story of the golden arm and began to ask if anyone knew if someone had stolen it. Everyone he asked sent him to someone else. The first people he asked were the two thieves, but of course they didn't know anything about the golden arm. "Go ask so-and-so, he will know." But so-and-so didn't know, and sent the policeman off to ask someone else. "Ask him. He will know." Always it was someone else who was sure to know, and the policeman never did find out who stole the golden arm.

THE BOX

A surprise story that delighted children in Barrington was about a man who was given a large box. He carefully opened it and found inside another box. He opened it and found inside another box, and on and on, he went opening boxes each a little smaller than the one before until he came to a very tiny box. He opened it and out jumped, "*Boo!*"

◆ GAMES ◆

Among the games known and played by the children of Shelburne County, there are variants of traditional games passed on by generations of children to their successors. Others are of more recent origin, some improvised by children "just for fun." Among the many indoor games are Hide the Thimble, Guess the Word, and My Aunt's Just Come from Boston.

HIDE THE THIMBLE

The one chosen to hide the thimble puts it in an inconspicuous place, but plainly visible, while the other players "hide their eyes" or leave the room. When the thimble is hidden the player calls, "Beans and brown bread come to your supper." To find the location of the thimble, the players keep asking, "Am I close?" The one who has hidden the thimble replies, "hot," if very close, "cold," if far away, "cool," if near. The first to see the thimble sits down and is the next to hide the thimble.

GUESS THE WORD

One person thinks of a word that the others must guess. On the blackboard, or on a large piece of paper, the one chosen to select a word, writes a dash for each letter. Someone asks, "Is the first letter such and such?" If wrong, the player at the blackboard draws a circle for the head of a man. Another guesses a letter. If correct, it is marked in the space indicated; if wrong, the ears are drawn on the head of the man—and so on. If the player gets the man drawn before the others guess all the letters, she wins.

MY AUNT'S JUST COME FROM BOSTON

All players sit on chairs in a circle. One says to the player next to her, "My aunt's just come from Boston." She is asked, "And what did she bring you?" "A fan," waving her hand as a fan. The game goes on until all have stated, "My aunt's just come from Boston," and all are waving a hand for a fan. Then the first to start the game, again says, "My aunt's just come from Boston." And is asked, "What did she bring you?" "A fan and a pair of scissors," clipping two fingers of one hand and waving the other for the fan. Finally, "My aunt's just come from Boston. And, "What did she bring you?" "A fan and a pair of scissors and a hobby-horse," rising and bobbing as if on a hobby horse.

Among the many outdoor games are two that a little girl in Welshtown played: Mumbly Peg and Bobby Lingo.

MUMBLY PEG

Mumbly Peg was played with a hat pin or a three-pronged fork over a bed of moss. The terms were:

Front hand—*the pin flipped from the palm of the hand.*
Back hand—*the pin flipped from the back of the hand.*
Flap Jack—*the pin held on a finger and flipped over.*
Fister—*the pin placed on the fist and flipped over.*
Elbow—*the pin placed on the elbow and flipped over.*
Over shoulder—*the pin flipped over the shoulder.*
Knee—*the pin flipped from the knee.*

BOBBY LINGO

The game is played with the children in a circle, hand in hand. One goes around the circle saying, "Who goes around my stoney wall?" The others answer, "None but Bobby Lingo." Tapping each in the circle, the one going around the wall says, "One by one, two by two, come out here Bobby Lingo." The child who is tapped on the word "Lingo" leaves the circle. This is repeated until only the last two who then lift their arms in an arch for the others to pass under, asking of each, "Would you rather have a cake or cookies?" When all have chosen "cake" or "cookies" the game ends with a tug of war. Whichever side falls down first, the others shout "rotten egg."

SALLY IN THE SAUCER

This is a game the children in Green Harbour like to play. The children form a ring around "Sally" who is crouched down weeping. They sing:

Sally in the Saucer, wipe away your tears.
Turn to the right, turn to the left,
Turn to one that you love best.

Sally wipes away her tears; turns to the right, turns to the left, and turns to the one that she loves best—who is then Sally in the Saucer.

STEAL GOLD

For this game, long popular in the Barrington-Hibbards Brook schoolyard, a line is drawn across the yard. In each section is a pile of rocks (gold). The captain of each section chooses his team, and appoints two gold tenders. The object of the game is to steal the other team's pile of gold by raiding their yard. Anyone tagged by a gold tender becomes a member of that side, and anyone he or she subsequently tags from the other side also changes teams. The game ends when all the gold is in one pile.

BOWLING WITH MARBLES

At the Hawk, children used empty cartridges for bowling pins and rolled marbles as if they were balls to knock them over.

LEAP-FROG

To leap-frog, one child crouches down; a second runs, and placing his hands on the back of the "frog," leaps over him, runs a few feet ahead and crouches down. A third boy does the same, leaping over the first and second "frogs." This continues until all the players are crouched down as "frogs." Then the first boy leaps over all the frogs, one by one, and takes his place at the head of the line—and so on until all are tired of leap-frog.

FOXES AND HOUNDS

The little one and two-roomed schoolhouses set among pastures and woodlots, such as the Hibbards Brook school, were the ideal settings for playing foxes and hounds. Two or three children were designated hounds; the others, the foxes, started off ahead of the hounds and were given time to spread out across the fields and into the trees. There, they marked their trail with broken branches, until they came again to open pastures. If the hounds were pressing close, they scattered to hide behind rocks or bushes and tried to elude the hounds. Those tagged by the hounds were out of the game; those that returned to base shouted, "One, two, three, I'm free."

◆ CRAFTS ◆

ALDER WHISTLES

In the spring, when the sap flows in the long stems of alder, and the bark can be removed with gentle pressure, the season for alder whistles has arrived. In a straight, finger-thick length of alder, the points of the whistle are cut and with gentle tapping the bark removed to shape the mouth piece. For a day the whistle responds to the eager puffs blown into the pipe; then, it is dry and soundless and a new whistle has to be made.

THE CHESTNUT PIPE

When chestnuts lie on the ground, it is time to make a chestnut pipe. Scoop out the center of the chestnut, drill a hole in one end and insert a dried stalk of goldenrod for a stem. Fill the bowl with dried fern or shreds of old man's whiskers and light up for one puff of smoke.

CUSTOMS AND CELEBRATIONS

◆ HOME CUSTOMS ◆

In addition to brewing home remedies on the kitchen stove, ink, dyes, soap, paint, paste, and glue were also prepared in the home. These domestic recipes and skills were passed down to the next generation and still remembered by some mothers and grandmothers, fathers and grandfathers.

SOAP MAKING

Soap making was an important household activity. In a wooden tub beneath the dry sink in the back entry, bones and scraps of fat were collected to be boiled in lye into hard tallow soap, "taller soap." For soft soap, cracked bones and marrow were dissolved in a tub of lye, making a soft, viscid solution that was used to scrub wooden floors and tables.

Gurry soap was made in the fishing villages from barrels of fish offal, saved by the fishermen to grease the skidways beneath their boats when winching them ashore. The lye was leached from wood ashes that were soaked in a barrel with a hole in the bottom to drain the lye. The gurry and lye were boiled together until the mixture would float an egg or a potato, when it was "strong enough" to make hard soap.

PAINT

Paint for houses was made of red or yellow ochre, slaked lime and oil, and was mixed with fresh skimmed milk if it was to be used indoors on walls and woodwork. A man who lived at the Hawk, near Clarks Harbour, remembered using red ochre mixed with oil to paint his house, and painted the roof shingles with seal oil and red ochre. A good paint for houses and fences was a mixture of rosin melted in oil, added to milk and slaked lime. Another paint for the roof was made of fine sand, ashes, and slaked lime, mixed with oil. It was applied to the shingles with a wide brush—first coat thin, second coat thick. For those who lived in Jordan Falls, a good source of red ochre was "up the tote road west of the river."

Many houses and outbuildings were whitewashed with slaked lime in which glue from a fish skin was added. For white paint, quarts of white lead were stirred with oil in wooden tubs.

PASTE AND GLUE

Wallpaper paste was made by boiling flour and water. Homemade glue came from fish skins, cod and cusk providing the best.

INK AND HOMEMADE DYES

Good black ink was brewed from inkberry, *Ilex glabra*, and from maple bark. The same berries were used to make black dye, as was alder bark. Seaweed was gathered for a brown dye, and for yellow, onion skins were boiled. Lichens gave various dyes: "cockles" from maple trees provided a rich brown colour; old man's whiskers, a light sand or beige; rock cockles, light brown; and the stiff, shell-like rock lichen, a deep rose. Navy-blue dye was boiled from logwood brought from the West Indies in homeward bound vessels. To set the colours of homemade dyes, either a small lump of rock alum, salt and vinegar, or urine was added to the dye pot.

The natural colour of yarn spun from the wool of brown sheep was known as "heather" or "burnt"; "clouded" yarn was strands of yarn dyed different colours.

SPINNING AND WEAVING

In some homes there were looms, spinning wheels and "winding blades," to wind yarn into skeins. Cloth was woven for clothing and blankets, and for rugs to cover the bare floors. A single strand of yarn as it came from the spinning wheel was known as "open-banded"; for two-ply yarn, it was "double-and-twist"; for three-ply, "treble-the-three." Yarn spun from wool sheared from sheep that roamed their home pastures was known as "homeste'd"; clothing made from the yarn was known as homeste'd clothing. Those who remembered their grandmothers weaving yards of heavy cloth for pants and coats, remembered "plain weaving" had two threads; "swansdown" had four threads. Women went from house to house spinning for two cents a skein and weaving blanket cloth for seven cents a yard. One young widow, in Brass Hill, "buckled to" and made a living for her children weaving rag rugs. They were laid on the floor of the front room over a layer of oat straw. "Ingrain" carpets were woven in a pattern "one colour on top; another beneath," red above, gold beneath.

MATS

Mats were hooked of wool or of rags. Heavy rag mats were hooked on crocus bagging, the coarse burlap of oat or middling bags. A sturdy scatter mat for kitchen floors was a "sheeny mat," a "hit-and-miss," hooked of bright coloured rags, each row a different colour. A favourite design traced on burlap to be hooked in wool or finely cut rags, was of roses, thistles, and shamrocks within a border of scrolls, and against a "main" or background of grey, sand, or brown.

A coin mat was made with circles of flannel traced around coins that were feather-stitched in various designs onto squares of woolen cloth. The squares, feather-stitched together with a backing of blanket cloth, made an attractive bedroom mat.

Painted canvas mats were made for back entries and sinkrooms. Flour and cold water were mixed and boiled to a smooth paste that was brushed over the canvas. When dry, it was painted with odds and ends of house paint, with brightly coloured designs, bursting red roses, scrolls and geometric patterns, or a ship in full sail. Sometimes, yellow or red ochre paint was painted on the canvas as a background for the design.

QUILTS

Patchwork quilts, like hooked mats, were a part of home life. Their bright blocks of squares were sewn together according to a design, such as "crazy quilt," "hole-in-the-wall," "wedding ring," or "Star of Bethlehem," and many other designs. Quilted to a lining, through a cotton or woolen bat, or, as was discovered in Lockeport when a century-old quilt was repaired, through a bat of newspapers, they made warm bedcovers.

Bed ticks were stuffed with hay, oat, or barley straw, or with eelgrass, where oats or barley could not be grown. Thus the old command, "Com' on boy, 'tis time to get in your eelgrass." Those who had hay-filled ticks were told "to hit the hay."

A family in Welshtown used to sit around the kitchen stove on winter evenings stripping fine strips of birch from birch sticks to be used to stuff their bed ticks. In spring, the old crushed birch strips were thrown away, and the new ones were stuffed into freshly washed bed ticks, starched stiff with flour paste. Over the birch tick was a feather tick. In the winter those high-mounded ticks were warmed with peeled sticks of wood scorching hot from the oven or hot stones wrapped in flannel.

WITHEROD BASKETS

Baskets were woven from long slender rods of witherod and were used aboard fish boats; smaller witherod baskets were used to carry fish ashore. For a housewife, fish could be easily washed in a witherod basket, for the loosely woven strands permitted the water to flow through. The farms in Ohio used witherod baskets when harvesting crops of potatoes.

WATER DIVINING

For years one water diviner found springs of water with the forked bough of an apple tree. One spring he found in Shelburne, many years ago, is still filled with water in the summer, when wells all around are dry.

FOODS

Many foods and old rules (recipes) for cooking, although not part of today's fare, are still remembered. For many, food was the product of their labour. Along the shore, fish, clams dug from the sand flats, lobsters, such as an old man of Cranes Point remembered he used to find hidden beneath the rocks in shallow water, were staple fare. Those who lived inland, remember moose muffle, a stew made from the flesh around a moose's nostrils.

In areas of rocky soil, where many lived, only barley could be grown to be ground into flour in the grinding mill. For barley bread, yeast had to be made from hops that grew over stonewalls or outbuildings. Yeast was also made from potatoes. In Shelburne, an old lady sold her yeast for five cents a cup.

An old custom in Sandy Point when baking bread was to bake an extra loaf to give to a friend. The bread was baked in the morning, with the breakfast fire, and a warm loaf was left at a friend's door.

Hot steamed brown bread of cornmeal and molasses was a stand-by for breakfast. Oatmeal, as a hot breakfast in the summer was frowned upon by those who considered it "too hot for the blood," and said that it caused salt rheum and blisters on the hands. For some, breakfast was not complete without a wedge of gingerbread soaked in cream, or a piece of pie. For a special Saturday night supper, there was steamed brown bread laden with "sticky raisins" and beans baked in a crock with fat salt pork and molasses.

Pork cake and Washington pie, a layer cake spread with raspberry jam and covered with whipped cream, were favourite cakes. "Patty cakes," "patty pans," and cup cakes were nicknamed "dory plugs." "Johnny cake," or as some called it, "hoe cake," made of cornmeal and molasses, was served hot from the oven; "dunky flunk," leftover pie crust cut in strips, was baked and broken into small pieces.

As well as pies for dessert, there were puddings—Indian pudding made of corn meal, molasses, and ginger, and caramel custards flavoured with burnt sugar, Irish moss pudding cooked until thick in a double boiler, and beesling pudding made from thick fresh milk from a cow "just freshened," which, with an egg added, looked like yellow cheese. When making cakes, pies, and puddings with eggs, the shells must never be thrown away until the dish is in the oven, for fear of bad luck.

Early each spring, patches of barren ground were burned over for blueberries; where there was kilkid, blueberries refused to grow. For winter use blueberries were either dried, or stewed and "put down" in narrow-necked crocks covered with brown paper made airtight with melted paraffin wax poured over the paper. Fresh blueberries were made into pies, "blueberry buckle," stewed blueberries with dumplings or dough boys, and "blueberry fungy," a word that perhaps comes from "spongy," for the dough of the fungy as it steams becomes light and spongy. Besides the drying of blueberries for winter use, apples were pared and sliced and strung on long loops of string and hung from rafters to dry.

Steak and stew meat inclined to be tough was "stifled," "muddled," or "smothered." "To stifle meat put it in a pan and sear it some. Make some gravy and put the cover on."

From Bon Portage came a recipe for "tatter toddle" (which was known in Welshtown as "toddle potatoes").

"Cube meat and salt pork; cube turnips and potatoes and slice onions. Add water and cook."

"Cracklin," a well known Shelburne dish, was made of salt pork scraps, fried until they crackled, and were added to salt fish.

Most families had a pork barrel filled with salt pork, and some had smoked moose meat that they chipped or sliced thin for special dishes. Moose meat and deer meat were also pickled or salted in barrels in the cellar. Bacon was a special treat, especially when made into "devil-a-horse-back"—chips of fried bacon on cheese and toast baked in the oven.

TEAS, CORDIALS, WINES, AND SYRUP

Teas, cordials, wines and syrup were made from leaves and flowers, from vinegar, molasses, and oatmeal. In Jordan Falls a favourite drink on a hot summer day was "vinegar fizz," made of vinegar in a glass of soda water. "Oatmeal drink" made of oatmeal, brown sugar, vinegar and ginger, and teaberry cordial, made from checkerberry (wintergreen) leaves, with a little sugar and vinegar to draw out the juice, were also favourite drinks. A mild tea was steeped from the leaves of Labrador tea and from the leaves and blossoms of bunchberry. Blueberries and dandelions were brewed into wines, vigorously frowned upon by teetotalers. As sauces for puddings there was treacle, also used as a spread on slices of bread, and a syrup made of molasses and melted butter flavoured with maple.

For raspberry leaf tea there was an old blessing:

For what we have,
We give unto thee,
Fish and potatoes,
and raspberry leaf tea.

♦ *SOCIAL CUSTOMS* ♦

Social activities that bring friends together are important to a community's past and present, but some social customs are now only memories of the past.

Many events centered around work: knitting and spinning parties; quilting bees and mat hooking, which women were told brewed bad weather. A woman might walk long distances to spend the day knitting with a friend. Later, she would return home in time to milk the cow and house her roaming flock of hens.

Men had chopping and digging contests. To clear a garden plot in Oakpark, a farmer marked off the land to be made ready for his garden and divided the plot into equal sections, one for each man. He set a jug of rum a certain distance down the rows. The first man to dig to the jug had the first swig of rum; the others took their swig as they came to the jug. Then the jug was moved further down the line, and the men dug on, each receiving his reward until the garden was ready for seeds and the jug of rum was empty.

A home custom among the descendants of the Welshtown settlers was "dinner-bah" and "supper-bah." Each morning everyone stopped working and gathered with others for dinner-bah, a cup of tea. Again, in the afternoon, they gathered for supper-bah.

There were many evenings with lively games of My Aunt's Just Come From Boston, The Whispered Tale, How the Story Grew, Musical Chairs, and Find Your Lover in the Dark. There were parlour sing-songs, and singing schools on winter evenings.

The popular game of 45s has a vocabulary of words and expressions and ways to entice good luck which make it a lively game. The ten of clubs—"old mossy face"—is also known as the "devil's woodpile," "black huckleberries," "fruitcake," and "blanket." The jack of hearts is a "hefty man from Birchtown"; the two of trumps is the "saucey two" or "Nellie's hat." "Big Cassey" is the ten of diamonds; "five fingers," the five of trumps. Cards "with eyes" are the kings, queens and jacks. A "kicker" is a small trump card that will force the bidder to play a high trump; a "soup card" is any card not a trump that takes a trick. The five of trumps is the "roof"; other high trump cards, the "rafters." On a weak bid, even a small trump will "take the roof"; a high bid on a weak hand is "Joe Bluff." When trumps are named by a player, for instance "hearts," the player would say, "hearts are the good ones, bay rum," with a good trill to the rum.

To change the luck, the cards are given an Irish or a Scotch poke, or are passed around a chair leg, or the player walks around the chair. Even better, sit on a handkerchief or put on the "huckleberry" or the "ack-ah-loosa." A good firm tap with the cards against the right elbow for ack-ah-loosa, and against the left for huckleberry. Sometimes all that is needed is to change your "tick tacks" or play "cagey." If you are having good luck the devil's at your elbow.

Score-keeping has its terms: "below deck" or "in the cellar," a minus score; "above deck" is a "nest egg," a score of five, which is better than a "goose egg," zero when "even with the board." A score of 100, "You're on an island. We have the boat." With a score of 100, the bid must be twenty, and the others will play to "dreen" the bidder and make him "play turkey." A good trump played will "thicken the soup," "bring you to gaff." Sometimes the deal is "la-la-puloosa," a happy full hand of high trumps and the "devil takes the hindermost."

Outside the home, "Lantern Views," as one diarist of Little Harbour wrote in the 1890s, were popular entertainment, accompanied with a lecture from the minister. Pie sales were a means of earning money for schools and church, as were garden parties and tea meetings.

Homespun concerts were eagerly awaited entertainment. A production of local talents, skits and plays, verses and songs was assembled to amuse an audience that could enjoy its own foibles. Historical pageants commemorated the highlights of past years as a background for the present.

Horse-racing, frowned upon by many, was a popular sport on the beach at Lockeport and at Barrington, near the Villagedale sandhills, until the early 1920s. The greatest attraction for years was the Temperance Picnic at Port Clyde where hundreds of temperance workers gathered, as well as many who were not "quite so strong for temperance."

COURTSHIP AND MARRIAGE

An old courtship custom remembered at Clarks Harbour was a true lover's knot, sent by a young man to the girl of his choice. Below a loop of twine, he tied a square knot, and an inch or two below it, a slip knot. If the young lady accepted him as her sweetheart, the lover's knot was sent back to him with the slip knot pushed against the square knot; if she wished their friendship to remain unchanged, the loop was returned as he sent it to her—the slip knot well below the square knot. If she wished to break their friendship, the slip knot was untied and the loop returned to the disappointed young lover.

Making a ring from a piece of girl's hair, to be worn

by her lover, is an old custom. A locket with a piece of a lover's hair, or a lock woven into a bracelet, are long remembered rituals of youth. Engagement rings were set with gems other than opals, unless the girl's birthday was in the month of October for whom opals are good luck. For others, opals bring sorrow and tears.

Showers of gifts for the bride were, and still are, held prior to, or following the wedding. In some communities, the bride walks around the room thanking each giftgiver. Then the bride and groom walk down rows formed by the men and women, the men kissing the bride, the women, the groom. Or, the men line up on the bride's side of the table, and the women on the groom's side to congratulate and kiss the bride and groom. In an old saying, the number of holders given the bride at her shower foretells the number of children she will have.

The old custom of a midnight shivahree for the bride and groom on the first night in their home, included the firing of guns and tooting of horns until the wedding couple appeared, and were greeted with good wishes for happiness for their future.

FUNERALS AND BURIALS

Reaching back into the past, an old woman of Clarks Harbour related to her grandson the funeral and burial customs of her youth.

In earlier times, the sick and dying were cared for by friends and relatives in their homes. There were no undertakers, and a friend laid out the deceased in a coffin made of pine boards fitted with metal handles and a coffin plate. The lid of the coffin was secured with silver-coloured thumbscrews. It was carried to the church on a bier—a short-legged hand-barrow that stood on the ground beside the open grave. The underbearers carried it either on their shoulders or by hand. Over the coffin was a pall of black cloth, bound with tassels, which were held during the funeral procession by women pallbearers, who walked beside the coffin. Behind the bier walked the friends and relatives of the deceased. It was considered sinful to go fishing on the day of a funeral, even by men in another community. At the hour of death the passing bell was tolled, its muffled strokes marking the number of years in a deceased's life. The bell was again tolled as the body was carried from the house to the church, and from the church to the burial ground.

Other people remembered different facets of funeral and burial customs. For some time after undertakers were available, the deceased continued to be laid out by a friend. Pennies were placed on the eyelids to hold them closed. When the hour of death seemed imminent, and coincided with the ebb-tide, when, it was believed, the strength of a sick person was ebbing, friends gathered in the house to await the passing of their friend. Old tales linger of those long hours of vigil. One tells of a clock that stopped when a man lay at the point of death. Then its heavy pendulum began to swing and he lived on—only to die the following evening at the same hour that the clock had stopped on the previous night.

At the time of death, the deceased's house was marked with a palm branch or a rosette of black crepe hung on one side of the front door. Funerals were often held in the home, in the front parlour, amid a great display of emotional distress. For a year following a death, mourners wore black, a widow a long veil edged with black, and black crepe armbands were worn by both men and women. Other symbols of mourning were black-edged handkerchiefs and black-edged writing paper, and in the local newspaper a band of black enclosed what in some papers was listed as the Death Roll. Mourning continued for a year. It was considered a breach of respect for the departed if either a widow or a widower remarried before the expiration of a year following a loved one's death. Before burial, the coffin plate engraved with the deceased's name, date of birth and death, was removed from the coffin and mounted on velvet, sometimes with a lock of hair, and framed, to be hung as a momento in the parlour.

To toll a bell, a man in Shelburne remembered, it was one clap every two minutes for half an hour.

In at least in one small community, there was a pauper's lot outside the wall of the burial ground for those who could not afford a lot inside the grounds.

◆ *DAYS OF CELEBRATION* ◆

CHRISTMAS

In "bon auger days," the good old days, Santa Clausing or Santy Clausing began with Christmas Eve and continued for the twelve days of Christmas, to old New Year's. Santa Clauses were always dressed in costumes and carried a bag for the cakes and cookies, known as "santys," given them for their singing and dancing. In an 1895 diary, it was reported that on Christmas Eve in Little Harbour, "We had a call from four black boys for sandy's this evening." Santa Clausing was common throughout Shelburne County, especially on Cape Sable Island and in Lockeport, where it was prepared for weeks in advance, and where it was practised long after it had ceased in other communities. Poems and stories were recited celebrating some event in the neighbourhood or about a person in the community, and little plays presented in the kitchens of the homes they visited, where they also stepdanced and played tunes on Jew's harps, combs and whistles. In anticipation of their arrival, plates of santys were prepared on Christmas Eve and in the evenings following. As with many old customs, only a part remains: Santa Clauses, dressed for the evening in old clothes and with a bag for treats, occasionally come to the door nowadays on Christmas Eve.

In bon auger days, stockings were hung up on Christmas Eve to be filled by Santa Claus. They were also hung up on New Year's Eve, which was known as old Christmas, for Kris Kringle, Santa Claus's brother to fill, and again a week later, on Old New Year's to be filled, it was hoped, by someone.

Stockings were filled with raisins, figs, and nuts, a bag of candy, an orange in the toe, grapes on top, and a horn picture book, its parchment pages protected by a sheet of horn, shaved thin. One man remembered that there was always a potato and a piece of coal in his Christmas stocking. On New Year's, the stockings had nuts, figs, dates, and money in the toe, for a prosperous year ahead. There was little in the stocking on old New Year's—just an orange or an apple.

Christmas trees were not popular until the turn of the century. In some families, the tree was not brought in the house until Christmas Eve, after the children were in bed. To decorate the tree, there were candles in clip-on sconces, a few bright balls and ropes of cranberries, rosehips, and popcorn, strung by the children sitting in the evenings around an oil lamp. For a few years, there were sparklers, looking like silver rods hanging from the branches, that burned with bright sparkles when touched with a lighted match.

Handkerchiefs were a popular gift, and an old Christmas saying told that the number of handkerchiefs received, the number of years before a girl married.

NEW YEAR'S DAY

New Year's morning was an anxious time for those who feared a woman would be the first at their door, when for good luck through the year, it must be a dark-haired man. He is known as the "first footer." In one house in Shelburne, it was a custom to give a jackknife to the first boy who came to the door on New Years' Day. They never failed to have a boy waiting in the cold for the door to open.

To some, the New Year was a time to give small gifts to friends and relatives. On New Year's Eve, children went around dressed up, as on Christmas Eve, asking, "Have you anything for New Year's?" They wished the gift-givers a happy New Year.

To have something new all year round, something new, if only a handkerchief, must be worn or carried in a pocket on New Year's Day. To ensure a full cupboard all the year, an abundance of fruit and groceries were purchased and stored in bins for the New Year.

A late-night service was once the custom, with prayers to end the old, and begin the new. The church bell tolled the old year out and the new year in. Fire crackers and the firing of guns now mark the turn of the old to the new.

For men, the New Year's Goose Shoot is still a special event. The person with the highest target score wins the goose.

ST. VALENTINE'S DAY

At school, for St. Valentine's Day, hearts were cut from red paper and pasted on folded sheets of paper; bright pictures from Eaton's catalogue and magazines decorated the folded sheets, or pictures were drawn and verses written on the inner fold. One popular verse was:

Roses are red,
Violets are blue,
Sugar is sweet,
And so are you.

For weeks in advance, a decorated box waited in the schoolroom for the valentines as they were made by the children. On the long-awaited day, the box was opened and the teacher announced the names written on the valentines as she drew them from the box, and chosen couriers rushed about the schoolroom bestowing on each pupil a personal valentine.

EASTER

An old Easter custom among the boys in Shelburne was to go in the woods on Good Friday, sometimes on the further side of the harbour, and build a brush tent for an Easter camp. Here they had a picnic and played games and if it was warm, they slept there. Girls had their Easter camp nearer home and built it in the shape of a teepee. They had hard-boiled eggs and homemade bread with molasses for their picnic.

Decorating blown eggs was, and still is, an Easter custom. Hard-boiled eggs were painted in bright colours, and sometimes a girl's face was drawn on the egg and a sunbonnet tied beneath her chin. Designs from a piece of cloth could be imprinted on an egg by boiling it inside a tightly sewn bag of printed cloth.

Egg cracking was fun, each trying to crack the other's egg as they knocked them together. The first to crack the other's egg claimed the cracked egg. Of course, there were egg hunts, and challenges—"I bet a dollar you can't find my egg."

APRIL FOOL'S DAY

April Fool's Day was a morning for fun, for all pranks and jokes ended at noon or you were "the biggest fool at last." Long paper tails and April Fool placards were pinned on sweaters and skirts; and the unwary, forgetting the day, were fooled with, "Look at the bird," when there was no bird, and then dubbed an "April Fool." It was fun to say you had a secret to whisper in someone's ear, then instead, to blow in the ear and chuckle, "April Fool." In a small one-room schoolhouse all the children arrived early on April Fool's Day and stuffed the school bell with paper. When the teacher came to the door to ring the bell they all shouted, "April Fool."

MAY DAY

In Barrington, May Day baskets, made from paper and filled with flowers, were left on a friend's doorstep. On Cape Island, the children went into the woods on May Day morning and danced and sang among the trees.

ARBOR DAY

For days in advance, Arbor Day was looked forward to by school children as a day of busy fun. School rooms were scrubbed, desks polished, and windows cleaned by the girls, while outdoors, the boys laboured to sink rocks in the schoolyard, to dig a patch of ground for flowers, and plant trees. By noon, with windows shining and trees planted, there was a picnic followed by games and baseball.

HALLOWE'EN

Hallowe'en was the day that cabbages left in the garden disappeared. It was the day for Kalecannon—boiled cabbage, turnip and potatoes, mashed together with plenty of butter and served with sliced tongue. If there was a party, a ring and a thimble were added to the Kalecannon—a ring for a wedding—a thimble for an old maid.

Jack-o'-lanterns were made from boxes, and sometimes from small pumpkins. It was a night for "whiz buttons" and "jinny spinners," buttons and spools with string threaded through the holes, to be spun against window panes as jack-o'-lanterns grinned through the glass.

Apples were bobbed in large tubs of water, and fortunes were told from apple seeds, while long streamers of apple peelings were twirled three times around the head and tossed over the left shoulder to fall in the initial of a future lover. Apples were flicked with a forefinger and a wish made which would come true according to the number of seeds: this year, next year, sometime, never. Girls lowered the end of a ball of yarn down a well, and walked three times around the well chanting an incantation hoping to see their future husbands; and at the "witchy hour" (twelve o'clock on Hallowe'en night), they combed their hair standing in front of a mirror hoping to see their future husband, looking over their shoulders.

GUY FAWKE'S DAY

In Shelburne, Guy Fawke's Day, November 5, was celebrated at night with a bonfire and the burning of the Pope—a figure made of straw or of mud, thrown on the fire as everyone danced, and the boys jumped over the fire.

SEA LORE

◆ FISHING ◆

As part of that great "new founde lande" where, Jean Rotz noted in 1535, "men goeth a fishing," the shores of present-day Shelburne County were eagerly explored by fishermen and adventurers for new places to fish and for land where they could dry their fish. By 1563 they had marked on their charts a good place from which to fish and a good place to dry their catch—the long point of land they called Bacalhaos, the Portuguese word for dried cod fish.

Later, the abundance of fish off these shores brought the first permanent settlers: the early French fishermen, who founded small settlements along the coast from "Cap de Sable" to "Cap Nègre," at "Port Razair" (Shelburne Harbour) and eastward along the shores, in sheltered coves and inlets. Following the brutal expulsion of the French, their homes burned and their land devastated, the New England settlers came to fish and to found permanent communities. They built vessels to take their dried fish to their old New England homeports and to far distant seaports in the West Indies.

The New England settlers brought with them their traditional ways of fishing which had been passed from generation to generation. In their turn, on a new shore, they taught their sons how to fish, how to make "drails," and "killocks" (stone anchors), how to build fish boats. As the years have passed, most of the old ways of fishing have been replaced, but there still linger some of the traditions, passed on to each succeeding generation, as well as many of the old superstitions. These notes on sea lore have been provided by those who remembered the old ways of fishing, and by those who fish today.

◆

A little boy in Port Saxon in the 1870s went fishing with his father in his "pinkie" off Cape Negro, and, on their first night at sea, old man Neptune came on board with a bucket of sour yeast. It was sour hop yeast and Neptune lathered the boy's face with it. At night, in the wavering light of a candle stuck in a sticking tommy, "a sticking tom," a metal candleholder with two sharp-pointed arms to wedge into the hull or the deck of a vessel, the boy learned to chop bait and to bait fish hooks. He scooped water with a "scoot horn" (a cow's horn attached to a long pole) to wet the sails of his father's boat to catch a passing breeze, for wet canvas held more wind than dry; and his father would not let him whistle on board their pinkie for it would bring a gale of wind, "butt end fo'most."

◆

In the waters off Cape Sable, two young boys who lived near the Hawk Inlet went fishing with their fathers. They learned of sunken ledges and hidden rocks lying in the water off the cape, and that the best time to fish was on the ebb tide slack, when the water was motionless, as it was best to push off from the shore in a sailboat on the ebb tide and return on the flood. They watched for schools of fish: for herring that dimpled the water's surface like raindrops; for mackerel—like a squall of wind touching the water—"Come up black; then calm; come up black." They learned to watch the seabirds that follow schools of fish: gulls for herring and pollack, gannets for mackerel, hags for squid. They fished to "lur'd" to catch mackerel, for mackerel swim with the wind; herring against the wind. When pollack drove schools of smaller fish to the surface, the boys caught them with "drails" that they helped their fathers make from long-shanked fish hooks.

When they went offshore deep sea fishing, and hove to to find a "live bottom" of rocks and hard ground where there would be cod and haddock, they learned to "arm the lead line." They filled the hollow, cup-shaped recess in the lead weight with soap or butter to pick up sediment from the ocean floor. Standing at the starboard bow, they heaved the lead slightly in front of the bow to carry the rope to the bottom as their boat drifted slowly. When the lead came up with sand in the butter, they moved off to find a hard bottom, where there were long ribbons of weeds growing on the rocks and in the mud, where there were crustacea, algae, and other food for fish.

They knew the old story told on "the Island" of two boys who went fishing with a skipper who boasted he knew where he was by the smell of the mud that came up in the butter. To test their skipper they took on board a bucket of mud from a Clam Point mud flat. When it came their turn to heave the lead and line, they rubbed the butter in the bucket of mud and carried the lead to their skipper. He took one sniff of the lead and shouted, "Heave off, boys. We're on a Clam Point mud flat."

When they were older, one of the boys learned to scull and to fish from the stern of a dory. Standing at the stern, he sculled the oar lying in the notch cut in the transom with his right hand; with his left he measured out with the heave stick, the baited trawl line over the starboard gunwale. If there were two tubs of trawl, he measured the lines port and starboard. On a good day for fish, he caught them port and starboard, slatting them from the loaded hooks into his dory until it was heavy with fish.

They watched the wind to prove the old verse:

When the wind is in the east, the fish will bite the very least.
When the wind is in the south, the bait will fall right in the fish's mouth.
When the wind is in the west, fishing will be at its very best.
When the wind is in the north, never should a fisherman venture forth.

They were good days learning to fish when fishing was at its very best; and when it came a "lur'd day" and a fisherman should not venture forth, they helped their fathers knit nets to catch mackerel and herring, and dyed them in the great iron tan pots that stood on the shore near their father's fish houses. They learned to shape "bows" and "roundys" for lobster pots, and made stout buoys from heavy blocks of wood, painting them with seal oil and ochre and marking them with their father's symbols. Sometimes they made a "spin top," a buoy for a lobster pot, shaped like a top that spun and turned with the current. Along the shore they collected flat rocks for ballast in lobster pots and for "stone killets." With a jackknife, they whittled "thole pins" for dories and wooden pegs to drive into the claws of lobsters as they were lifted from the pots, and they learned to tie knots and to splice rope. It was a good life to be a fisherman and to know the ways of fish, and to be a skilled artisan, to shape and to make the tools of their trade, and to build boats—dories and skiffs—and to know how to sail them, how to row, and how to scull a dory.

◆

On the long shores of Sandy Point, washed with the waters of Shelburne Harbour, a little boy learned from his sea captain grandfather the different sounds of the sea: the uneven beat of the waves as they roll and break on the rocks; the long rippling sound, the rote of the bow wave of a passing ship as it sweeps along the edge of the shore.

As young boys went fishing with their fathers to learn the traditional ways of fishing from small boats on the inshore grounds, older boys were hired as "flunkies" or "red jacks" on salt-cod "bankers" where they learned fishing on the offshore grounds. One man from Clarks Harbour, who was on a salt-cod banker in the 1880s when he was fourteen, remembered the way they fished and cured their catch, and their life at sea.

Some the crew, he recounted, went off in dories; one man in a dory for handlining, two in a trawl dory for longlining. Those who stayed on board the banker fished from the deck. The skipper was on the quarter-deck, "forward of the main rigging" where he could watch for any danger that might menace their vessel or the dories fishing nearby. Then came the cook, "just aft of the fore rigging," and the crew along the deck ranging to the farthest berth "aft on the quarter deck." After long hours of handlining, and the dories returned laden with fish, the "dressing crews" prepared the fish for salting: the "throater," the "header," and the "splitter," served by the "idler," who kept the throater's tub filled with fish, kept water in the splitter's tub, and pitched the fish from the splitter's tub to the "salter's," in the hold of the vessel.

The days were long. Some of the crew had their berths aft in the captain's quarters; others, in the forecastle where the cook was boss. In the forecastle was the shack cupboard that the cook kept filled with food for a "lunch up" between meals, when the crews worked twenty hours out of twenty-four. In the 1880s "salt horse"(salt beef) and "hard tack" (hard, thick biscuits, as hard as a tack) were the main fare in the old salt-cod bankers.

◆

For a young man it was a great adventure learning to fish on a deep-sea banker, but not all young boys returned to their homeport without mishaps, as an old Barrington sea captain told in a story of his younger years when he, too, sailed on a deep-sea banker.

There had been many days of rough wind and heavy seas, and as they neared Cape Canso, they saw a derelict schooner and what they thought from a distance were men clinging to a rock, the surf washing over them. The captain of the Barrington fishing schooner, *Georgie Harold,* called for volunteers. True to the valour of those who sail the oceans, young men stepped forward to man the dories, one of them a young man from Barrington. As they came near the rock they saw the crew of the Yarmouth schooner *Twilight* clinging to a pole they had wedged into a crevice of the rock. As the men were drawn into the dories, the young man from Barrington noticed what he thought was a round rock covered with seaweed that lifted and fell with the tide. Then he knew it was a boy who had slipped into the water with the tide lifting his hair as it flowed over the rock. The young man reached down through the water and drew the boy up by the hair of his head into the dory.

Years later when he was no longer a young man sailing in a fishing schooner, but captain of a vessel sailing between Barrington and American seaports, he was in Boston and met a man with whom he stopped to talk. When the man heard he was from Barrington, he told him that as a youngster on a fishing voyage he was wrecked off the shores of Cape Breton and was rescued by a young sailor from Barrington who thought, at first, his hair was seaweed on a rock until he reached down through the water and drew him by the hair into a dory. It was a moment when two men stood in silence—the rescued and the rescuer.

◆

When men fished from small boats, their wives and daughters went to the shore to help them unload their catches and to "barrow them up" to the fish houses on handbarrows made from barrel staves nailed crosswise to two long shafts or poles shaped to fit the hands. Later, when the fish were ready to dry, they were carried to the "fish flakes," tall racks of laths erected on poles, spread with netting or spruce boughs. If it was good fish, it dried in the sun and wind "to the whiteness of a hoar's tooth." As the fish were headed, gutted, and split to dry in the sun, the "bloody offals" were set aside for "chum," bait to be cast on the water when chumming for pollack. As cod fish were "dressed," the livers were thrown into barrels for liver oil. "Gurry," the refuse from cleaning fish, was used to grease the skids of the boat haul, to ease their boats up and down the skids, or it was used to make gurry soap.

Shore land was alloted to most of the early settlers for fish houses and wharves. Sheltered inlets and "shallop harbours" where small boats could be moored away from the wind and the breaking surf, were eagerly sought by fishermen. Here they built their "blockings and stores," small wharves and boat landings of stones held in a cribwork of logs, or of upright logs and a plank walkway, with a store at the head of the blockings for storage of gear, and a place to repair and make nets, drails, stone anchors, swivels and sinkers for fish lines, and later, as a place to make lobster pots. When larger boats were built, larger wharves were constructed of heavy logs and crib work, topped with planks edged with a squared timber top cap, and spiles for mooring of boats.

"Drails," made by a man in Sandy Point, whose grandson remembers watching the man's strong hands, were made of long-shanked fish hooks, seven or eight inches long. Two of the hooks he set in a mould, and poured hot lead over them. From a fruit can he cut a strip tin and wrapped it about the shank of the drail to attract the eye of a pollack. Today, long-shanked hooks, covered with rubber, are used for handlining or jigging for cod.

The same man had a "compass house." He had made it of a box with a hinged cover. Inside the box was divided with a glass partition. On one side was his compass, on the other, a candle or lamp he could light at night to watch the needle of his compass.

On a high shelf in an old fish house in Sandy Point, a sailor's "ditty-box" was stored. It was made of smooth wood painted green and had a sliding cover. When it was taken off to sea, it held the sailor's tools, and on the return voyage, it was filled "with pretty trinkets for his girl." Sometimes it was a "ditty-bag" a sailor carried over his shoulder filled with his personal belongings, and his tools to mend nets or splice rope.

◆

"Jigs," "mackerel bobs," and "swivels" were made by the fishermen: jigs of wires, seized to a bar of lead, were bent into hooks and baited with red flannel to catch squid; mackerel bobs, a lead with a hook, sometimes "bobbed" more sculpins than mackerel; swivels for codlines were cut from horn softened in warm oil.

Mackerel drifting was one way of netting mackerel. At night, the fishermen pushed offshore to the spawning grounds and set their long strings of nets from the bows of their boats, the inner end of the net moored to the bow, the outer end attached to a float with a lighted lantern as a marker. All night they drifted with the wind and the tide, and with daybreak they drew in their nets hopefully burdened with mackerel.

The nets were knit of string with a bag or net needle, whittled by fishermen from thin strips of wood. They were knit in a three-and-a-quarter-inch mesh for mackerel, two-and-a-half-inch mesh for herring. To tan-dye the twine and hide the nets from the sharp eyes of the mackerel and herring, and to preserve and strengthen the twine, the nets were dipped in a solution brewed from oak bark, or the buds and twigs of conifers, in the great iron tan pots beside their fish houses. Later, "cutch" (catechu) purchased from the merchants was used to tan the nets.

Stone anchors, called killets, killicks, or killocks, were

made of heavy stones wedged into a framework of wood, or the stones were held with pliable sticks bound together at the top and fitted to crosspieces of wood. "Scrodgers" were made from old crankshafts welded to an iron bar with a ring attached. They were used to snag things from the ocean bottom, especially anchors. "Grapnel," "graplin," a lightweight anchor used to moor small boats and nets, and to drag and "grapple" with objects on the ocean floor, was made of five or six iron hooks welded to an iron shank fitted with a ring. A "jone-post," used for mooring small boats and fishnets, was a weighted log set with a ring to which the painter from the bow is attached.

To "tail" an anchor, the rope was tied to the shank, near the arms, carried up the shank and tied with a bit of yarn (tailing) to the ring. If the anchor caught on the rocks or in the ocean-bed, a quick jerk of the anchor-rope broke the tailing and the rope upended the anchor, releasing it from the rocks.

As men worked in their stores, on their fishing gear, wives and mothers knit, as some do today, socks and heavy mitts, "nippers" and "wristers," and "thumb and finger stalls" of white yarn. Nippers, worn to protect the palm of the hand when handlining, were knit like the leg of a sock, doubled from both ends to the middle and padded with cotton for extra protection from the wet lines. Finger and thumb stalls, worn to protect a cut or wounded finger or thumb, were knit like the thumb and fingers of a glove. Wristers, knitted cuffs of white yarn, were worn about the wrists to prevent pingeons, the painful white sores caused by salt water and the harsh chafing of oilskin jacket sleeves against the wrist. Lacking wristers, a fisherman of Sandy Point wore seven links of chain about his wrist, and a man who fished from the shores of Cape Island, wound white yarn around and around his wrists.

As a cure for pingeons, wrists were rubbed with kerosene or creosote. When rheumatism plagued fishermen at sea, they dipped a bucket of salt water on the ebb tide and soaked their feet and legs to relieve the pain. Or, they made an ointment of grease—"Bair's grease if you could get it"—turpentine, and liquid ammonia, beat up with the white of an egg.

The waterproof oilskin jackets that irritated a fisherman's wrists were locally made of cotton, the garments, jackets, pants and sou' westers, cut and stitched by hand and waterproofed by soaking in tubs of raw linseed oil with boiled oil added to hasten the process of drying. "Barbels," long black waterproof aprons with a bib, held in place with a strap around the neck, worn by fishermen when fishing and when dressing fish, were also made of oilskin, lamp black or coal black added to the raw linseed oil for black oilskin. To prevent spontaneous combustion, the oilskins were hung on open racks, and never stacked in piles that might generate heat.

◆ *LOBSTERING* ◆

As ways of fishing have changed, so have the ways of lobstering. A lobsterman of Shag Harbour described how lobsters were first caught in "bow nets," each one made of an iron hoop, three or four feet in diameter, and a loose bag into which the lobsters fell when the hoop was lifted from the ocean floor. Three or four guy lines attached the hoop to a cork float and a rope that reached the surface of the water, where it was fastened to the top line. Some twelve or more bow nets were attached to the top line, which was held in place by anchor-fast moorings marked with buoys.

The same lobsterman remembered that the first lath traps were open at both ends, with twine-knit funnels, "potheads," through which the lobsters crawled to reach the "bait-spindle," a spike of wood baited with a knitted "bait-bag" stuffed with salt fish or with fresh bait punched down over the spindle. Later the construction of the traps was changed by "lathing-up" one end of the trap, and cutting two entrances, one on each side of the trap, with a pothead set with a "roundy," a "muzzle bow," made of pliable wood twisted into a loop. Fastened to one of the middle bows of the frame, a funnel enticed the lobster to crawl through into the lathed end of the trap, the "bedroom" or "parlour," where he could not escape. Still later, both ends of the trap were closed with laths and set with potheads inside the trap, and the lobster had the choice of entering the bedroom-parlour or the "kitchen."

At first, the traps were set on trawls, like the bow nets. Then, they were set singly with rope and a buoy and were known as "dump pots" as they could be dumped anywhere. The first pots were hauled on the slack of the tide "while under sail, or with small boats musceline was the motive power used." A "hurdy-gurdy," also called a "hurdy," a "line-hauler," a "hauler-head," or a "hand-hauler," which was a roller with a handle, made fast to the starboard gunwale, eased the weight of hauling nets and pots. A hurdy without a handle, a roller if made of dogwood (mountain ash), will keep evil spirits away.

When lobstering became more than a local enterprise, "lobster factories"(canneries) were built at the edge of the shore, extending out over the water. There were rooms for boiling and for packing, for cutting and rolling and soldering the tin cans for the boiled lobster meat, and for making the boxes in which the canned lobsters were shipped. In the "cracker room," the boiled lobsters were piled on tables, their shells cracked open, the meat pried from the shells and the empty shells tossed through "scuttle holes" cut in the floor into scows and towed offshore and shovelled into the ocean. Later, boxes, known as "cars," were filled with live lobsters and shipped to the American market in fast sailing vessels. In a few years came the lobster "smack," a sailing vessel fitted with a well filled with circulating water. To fill the smacks when they came along the shore, lobsters were held in floating lobster pounds to be transferred into the wells of the smacks.

◆ *BOAT AND SHIP BUILDING* ◆

As fishing gear and ways of fishing have changed, the fish boats have been reshaped, from the small, wind-driven shallops and pinkies of the early settlers, to the modern "Cape Island" motor boat, renowned and respected for its sturdy construction. As an early half-model of a "Cape Islander" built in Newellton in 1910 reveals, the early Cape Island boats were sharp and slender, with a long, narrow "counter," a small platform at the stern, which caused the boat to "hog" or bend upward in heavy seas. Year after year, new ideas were incorporated into the design, as the fishermen learned from experience the lines and contours needed in motorized fish boats to weather storms and heavy seas. The sharp, graceful lines gave way to a longer, wider boat, square-sterned, with a "cuddy"(cud) equipped with bunks and cook stove and an enclosed engine and wheelhouse.

As fish boats have been transformed, the dory, has been altered and enlarged as the "double dory," double in size to the smaller dory used for inshore fishing. Power dories, known as "long-liners," used on the bankers, replaced the smaller dories that were rowed. They were equipped with a power "gurdy" and were capable of handling five tubs of trawls. A mark of difference between Shelburne-built dories and those built elsewhere was a metal clip cut from galvanized sheet metal that joined the floor frame to the side frame, to which the pine planks were nailed. This replaced the "ship knees," the natural curved "knees" of hackmatack, cut from the roots and branches of the tree. A smaller dory used for inshore fishing, known as a "clipper," was also built in Shelburne. It had rounded sides rather than the slanted sides of the "bank dories," and, as its name suggests, it was fast moving and equipped with a sail.

The delight of children who lived on Green Island was to go "dory scudding" with their father, in the long rolling surf along the shore. Steering with a single oar at the stern, the dory was carried with the surf, like a surfboard.

Along with building small boats, the early settlers began to build brigs, brigantines, and schooners, using the oak, white pine, and hackmatack they cut in the nearby forest. From the days when sailing ships were built in the many shipyards that sprang up along the shores of the county are a few people who still remember the excitement of "launching day," when a ship went down the "ways" to meet the challenge of the sea. One old lady in Shelburne remembered, as a little girl, she learned to chant with the other children:

Wedge her up.
Out toggle,
Down dagger.
Hurrah!

A shipbuilder who launched many fine ships from his Shelburne shipyard used, "Out chisel, down dagger," as his command to release a ship, to slide with the "bilgeways" into the sea. "Dagger" is a shipbuilder's term for a "dogshore," a stout timber between the groundways and the bilgeways to hold a vessel steady while the keel blocks and shores are removed when launching the ship.

◆

An old man in Port Clyde used to delight his granddaughter with a story of a launching from his uncle's shipyard in Coffinscroft. Some of the young men took a bucket of rum along to the event and hid it behind the stone wall in the pig pasture. When all the "long faces" had departed, they started off for their rum. As they approached the wall, they heard the sound of a rumpus. When they reached the rum bucket, the pigs were rolling on their backs grunting and squealing, and two were fighting over the last drop in the bucket.

◆ *SEA STORIES* ◆

Some vessels were believed "witched" from the day their keel was laid until the day they sank beneath the waves. They were "joners," or "jonahs," from the very beginning and those who fished in them never filled their holds with fish. Sometimes there is a man on the vessel who is a jonah or even more distressing, one called a "decess." One fisherman in Ingomar believed he was a decess, and those who knew him believed so too, for when they were catching fish on every hook, if he came within a mile, "they would haul up bare and part off (rewind) the trawl."

The man had done very well fishing until he invested in a vessel built in Shelburne. "He went in over his head," and lost all his money. The vessel ended her days a rumrunner and he a decess.

Where there are shipyards, there linger stories of local ships. Tales of their adventures in faraway waters include mysteries that intrigue the imagination, bouts with pirates, along with stories of their hulls caught on their home shores. In recent times, there were the rumrunners, such as the *Nellie J. Banks,* built as a fishing schooner in Allendale, later used as a rumrunner. She was chosen as the symbol of the rumrunning days for a stamp issued in Saint-Pierre and Miquelon to mark the fiftieth anniversary of the end of prohibition in 1938.

◆

One acclaimed story is of the brigantine *Sebim,* built by Captain Warren Doane as his first adventure in shipbuilding. She was built on the eastern shores of Barrington harbour in the summer of 1849, and a few years later, in the summer of 1852, she was purchased by four of Captain Doane's brothers. They set sail for the gold fields of Australia, a long arduous voyage, and were rewarded in their search for gold. One of the brothers used the money he earned to study at the Royal Academy of Music in London. He later returned to Barrington and gave to his music-loving community the "gold of music," and began the research and writing of the history of Barrington Township. Two of his brothers also returned to Barrington; one remained in Australia and was for many years Mayor of Ballarat.

♦

The schooner *Vernon* carries a grim story of piracy and murder. She was built at Sandy Point, on the eastern shores of Shelburne Harbour, and proudly named *Vernon* by her builder and owner, Augustus Vernon. Three years later, in the early spring of 1840, she was chartered by a Halifax firm for a voyage to the West Indies. Her captain was James Cunningham of Churchover. Having delivered her cargo of salt fish, she was homeward bound, laden with puncheons of rum, when she was captured by a gang of pirates off the coast of Cuba. Captain Cunningham and two of his men were murdered, their bodies tossed into the sea. Young Benjamin Peach of Liverpool, managed to swim ashore, and after days of starvation, was rescued by the captain and crew of the schooner *Fauro* bound along the coast of Cuba.

Benjamin Peach could not speak Spanish, but he made the captain of the *Fauro* and his men understand that his ship had been captured by pirates, his captain and two others murdered. He had escaped and when the pirates came after him in their boat, he hid in a clump of reeds in a pool of water, and when they thrust their bayonets into the reeds they missed him by inches.

When they heard his story, the captain of the *Fauro* and his men were determined to capture the pirates. Guided by Benjamin Peach to the pirates' hideout, they pretended to be pirates and boldly rowed ashore. They told the ruffians that they knew of a vessel they could capture with their help and invited them on board the *Fauro* for dinner in the captain's cabin. When they were at dinner the door to the captain's cabin was closed and the pirates assured that if they made the slightest attempt to escape, they would be shot. Taken to Havana the pirates were condemned and hanged on the waterfront, their bodies left to swing in the wind, a stern warning to all would-be pirates.

◆

The unsolved mystery of the schooner *Blue Jacket* is not yet lost to local lore. She was built on John's Island at the mouth of the Sable River, by Josiah Pierce in the late 1860s. Her owner, Captain Colin Williams of Lockeport, used her for fishing and in the carrying trade, laden with barrel staves and lumber and fish for the West Indies, returning homeward bound laden with a cargo of sugar, rum and molasses.

On one of her long voyages she was sighted at a distance in the Gulf Stream by the crew of the *Jennie Hammond*, another of the old Lockeport sailing vessels. She looked strange to the seafarers, for there was no one at her helm, no one on deck, not even a shredded sail clung to her masts, and there was a slight slant to her hull. From the deck of the *Jennie Hammond* they launched a boat and boarded the *Blue Jacket*. They searched her from stem to stern but not a trace of the men who had sailed in her could they find. In this state she was a menace to ships, so they sank her in the Gulf, and returned to Lockeport to tell of the mystery that was never solved, for no trace of the six who had sailed in her was uncovered.

◆

In the spring of 1877, the *Codseeker* slipped down the ways from the shipyard of Thomas Coffin and Company, in Port Clyde. As her name suggests, "codseeking" was her destiny. On her maiden voyage she set sail for Halifax, for supplies, under the command of Captain Philip Brown. Laden with salt she turned her bow homeward for Barrington. Off the long point of Baccaro, struggling in a heavy southeast gale, she leaned far over on her side, and the loose salt in her hold shifted and held her on her beam ends. Three of her men, Captain Brown and two others escaped in a dory and reached the southern side of Cape Island, at Southside Beach, and carried word to Clarks Harbour. Captain Job Crowell and a crew of volunteers went out from there in the schooner *Matchless* to rescue those still clinging to the hull of the *Codseeker*.

Her men rescued, the *Codseeker* drifted off to sea. Several days later she was sighted by the American fishing schooner *Ohio*, drifting well off the shores of Seal Island. Some of the men of the *Ohio* rowed to the wreck and climbed up her rounded hull, and to their great amazement heard knocks from within. They hurried back to their vessel and told the captain she was haunted. He sent them back to the *Codseeker*, for if she was haunted they were living 'ghosts.' They cut a hole in her hull and lifted two men from the forecastle and brought them living to their homes, where their families were mourning their deaths at sea.

◆ *SHIPWRECKS* ◆

Tales of wrecks along the shores fill the annals of Shelburne County lore. Sometimes the name of the ship has been forgotten and only an incident remembered; for some, there are humorous tales; for others, there is the anguish of those waiting to be rescued, and the heroism of the rescuers.

◆

One shipwreck to be remembered above all others was the *Hungarian,* lost on a reef off Cape Sable on February 19, 1860. It was a stormy night, with fierce winds.

While one family waited for the birth of their firstborn child, they saw a red flare pierce the dark sky. Soon others who saw the red flares came to fetch the young father of the newborn baby to go with them to the shore and wait for the waves and wind to lessen so they could go out to the wreck. When daylight came, they saw the hull of a great ship leaning into the surf, and clinging to the hull and rigging those who had survived the night. As they watched they saw survivors falling into the sea, and when at last the force of the storm had lessened, and they manned their little boats, there was not a living soul clinging to the wreck. As many of the dead washed ashore, they were reverently buried in graves marked with field stones.

When searching for marks of identification, on one of the female passengers a diary was found, ending with the poignant words, "Lizzie dies tonight." From these words came a ballad, still remembered in part in the 1950s by an old lady who was six years old when the *Hungarian* fell beneath the waves. She learned all the verses when a child and sang, when she was ninety-seven, those she remembered.

Sad was our parting long ago
It gave us untold pain
But hopes were strong within our hearts
That we should meet again.

There's strength upon my cheeks once more,
And in my eyes new light.
And it will all be quenched in ocean's gloom,
For Lizzie dies tonight.

Lizzie dies tonight, mother,
Lizzie dies tonight.

The friends that loved you far away
Have guarded well your child.
They brought me almost back again
To you and home's delight.

Oh, I remember well the day,
When little Willie died
We laid him down with an aching heart
My father's tomb beside

It was then you filled my gentle heart
With prayers of pure delight.
I never shall repeat them more
For Lizzie dies tonight. ◆

Some stories of ships that caught their keels on the surf-lashed rocks and ledges have happier endings. A tale from Lockeport tells how the rescued and their rescuers stood on the shore and sang a hymn of praise and thanksgiving, led in their singing by the ship's band.

◆

East of Lockeport, a successful rescue through dense fog saved passengers and crew of the *City of Washington*, an iron-clad vessel on her way from Liverpool, England, to New York. When she struck a reef inside Port L'Hebert Rock, near Green Rock Bar, her captain thought he was many miles to the southwest, and that she had foundered on the shoals of Nantucket. When local residents heard the great boom of her hull against the rocks, they knew a large ship had grounded but through the great blanket of fog, lying heavy over the water, nothing could be seen.

Among those who heard the sound of her keel against the rocks was Cornelius Swansburg of Shelburne who was visiting relatives in Little Port L'Hebert on that day in July 1873. He ran to the shore to peer through the fog, accompanied by William Ferguson, who got up from his sick bed. Knowing of an old boat beached on the rocks, together, they pushed it off into the water, and as Ferguson bailed and guided their way through the fog, Cornelius Swansburg rowed. They shouted as they rowed, until at last, came an answering shout from the *City of Washington*. Out of the fog loomed her great iron hull, and from her deck her captain called, "Can you save these people?"

Assured that they could, boats were lowered, and, guided by William Ferguson, by nightfall all on board were rescued save the captain and a number of his officers who stayed with the wreck. Sails were brought from the *City of Washington*, and made into tents for the 567 people on shore. Ship's provisions were landed, and with food brought by local people, the night was passed in comfort.

The following day the fog lifted and Swansburg, with a crew of men, went out to the wreck for the captain and his officers. It was perilous rowing in the heavy seas now battering the *City of Washington*, crushing her broken hull. Less than a week later she broke amidships and most of her cargo was washed into the sea. In a few days, a ship came from Halifax for the passengers and crew.

◆

Less than a year from the day she was registered, the *Billow* caught her keel on Potters Ledge southwest of Ram Island and to the east of Lockeport. A splendid, two-masted brig, built in Barrington by John Lyle, she was on her way from Bermuda to Halifax under the command of Captain James Dennis of Yarmouth, one of her owners, when she was caught in a heavy gale off the coast of Nova Scotia and driven far off course. Some time in the night of April 9 she struck the outer rocks of Potters Ledge. In the pounding surf that broke her hull all on board perished—136 passengers, soldiers and officers of the 81st Regiment and their families, the captain and crew. The grief of that night of 1831 was caught in a poem by Almira Bell of Shelburne who lost cherished friends in the surf of Potters Ledge. Part of her poem reads:

List to yon sudden shock! yon long loud shriek!
What a sad tale of woe was chanted there!
When in one moment, brief as shadow's path,
Perished the young, the valiant with the fair.

Yes, all is past! the mad'ning waves around
Rush in with cruel and o'erwhelming sweep;
And faint as echo falls upon the ear,
Are hushed those sounds amid the roaring deep;
And buried with their bark, in ocean's wave,
Lie youth and age—the tim'rous and the brave.

◆

In Blanche, there is a story of a hero known as the "Little Irishman" aboard the American handliner, *Vinance*, which struck the southeast shore of Blanche Island, beyond the Salvages, in a blinding snowstorm in the winter of 1887. The place she struck was not far from the salt marshland that edged the shore of the island, but great waves rolled and broke against the *Vinance*. The Little Irishman told the captain he would take a line ashore. Struggling in the great waves, he reached dry land and set up a lifeline for all to come ashore—except two who, when the tide ebbed, walked to land. When men from Blanche reached the island on the ebb tide, all were safe, but the Little Irishman died from exhaustion in the bitter cold wind.

♦

One man from Blanche has a story he learned from his grandfather, who went out with others to bring ashore the crew and passengers of an immigrant ship that had come in behind the Half Moon (recorded on sea charts as the Salvages), and stranded on Flying Rock. When darkness fell they had rescued most on board. In the morning, they went back to the stranded vessel and found there was now one more on board than the evening before—a baby had been born during the night.

♦

The *Esme*, another ship wrecked at the back of the Half Moon, was on her maiden voyage, sailing in ballast from England to Saint John for a cargo of deals. All her crew was English except for one Portuguese. On that February morning in 1889, there was a strong southeast breeze. The man who first saw the wreck was made aware of something out beyond the shore when his dog kept sniffing the air and lifting himself up on his hind legs. As the darkness lifted, he saw the wreck and her distress signals. He went for the men of Blanche and they went out and rescued the men on board. Later, the Portuguese, with his arms hugging the warm stove, said, "If it weren't for that man then we'd all be sticking up our toes like dead dogs."

♦

In the winter of 1837, the *Amaranth*, bound for New York was forced onto the shores of Mud Island in a heavy storm. In some stories, all perished; in other tales, the captain and two of his men escaped. The corpses were buried by local inhabitants in shallow graves near where the *Amaranth* cast her keel. Years later, someone opened one of the graves, that of Margaret Flynn, from Ireland, and found her body had mysteriously turned to stone—to white marble, or as others say, to grey stone.

The story was told to a botanist-geologist making a floral survey of the islands along the shores of Cape Sable. As expected, on an island founded on granite, no hot or limestone springs, the usual causes of petrification, could be found.

◆

Beyond the long point at Blanche, the *Wildcroft* was making her way in dense fog into the harbour of Port La Tour when she struck land. Her captain believed, after days and days of fog, steering westward, that he had rounded Cape Sable and was safe in the deep water of the Bay of Fundy.

A boy, out in the morning fog, saw her great dark shape, and felt the crunch of her hull against the shore.

Then, out of the silence a voice called, "Ahoy."

The little boy shouted, "Hi."

The voice called again, "Where are we?"

The little boy shouted, "You're in Uncle Doug's potato patch."

It was early Sunday morning, a day to rest, a morning to sleep in. In a house above "Uncle Doug's potato patch" lived a fisherman and his wife. When the *Wildcraft*'s whistle sounded, he leaped out of bed shouting, "Land o' mercy, Marty, There's the trumpet! It's judgement day! Where are my pants?"

◆

From some of the many shipwrecks along the coast of Shelburne came new settlers. Among them was Captain Richard Hichens and seaman Thomas Middling of the brigantine *Friendship*. Laden with a cargo of sugar for Halifax in the winter of 1817, she struck a ledge off Cape Sable and drifted into a small inlet on the west side of the cape. Both young men married daughters of local families and founded families of their own. Richard Hichens and his wife Mary Crowell are remembered for their part in founding a lifesaving station on Seal Island, and Mary's name is enshrined in the Canadian Coast Guard search and rescue ship, *Mary Hichens*.

A Swedish vessel wrecked off Cape Sable brought James Obed and his wife to Blanche. Jacob Dixon, a native of Scotland, and Alexander Philips, shipwrecked off the shores of Cape Sable, settled on Cape Island and became teachers, Philips, an instructor in navigation.

One family shipwrecked near the Half Moon, in the ship, the *Proud Ardent*, remained as settlers. They were John Lainrock, a weaver from Ireland, his wife Betty and their son James.

◆

Hugh Crosby Kelly sailed as a young man from Ireland in the vessel *Merman* that was wrecked off Roseway. When rescued from her broken hull, young Kelly walked along the path from the beach to Nathan Doane's house, where he saw the pretty young Maria Doane drawing water from a well. They were married soon after and had a family of nine children. When Kelly died, his son Samuel was only nine years old, and his mother placed him with a family on Cape Negro Island. She soon learned that they were not good to him, forcing him to sleep outdoors beneath an overturned dory wrapped in a piece of canvas. She rescued him and took him to a friend, a captain of a whaler. Little Samuel cried bitterly as they sailed for Labrador and his homeland faded in the distance. The captain made him cabin boy, gave him the model of a little wooden boat to play with, and taught him to read and write. With never a day in school, before he was twenty-one he had passed his seaman's exams and was a master mariner.

◆

The story of John MacKenzie and his family, abandoned on the shore at Woods Harbour in 1795, is still remembered by their descendants. MacKenzie, a weaver from Scotland, was on an immigrant ship bound for America. The captain put into Woods Harbour to refill the water puncheons, and the passengers were told they could go ashore while this was done, but when they looked back to their ship, her sails were reset and her bow turned seaward. All they had were the clothes they stood in; the tools of their trades were gone with the ship. John MacKenzie, his wife and child, had nothing for their future but the guild papers for his trade. Some of the abandoned passengers found shelter in Woods Harbour, others, in Barrington. John MacKenzie first went to Port Joli, and later settled in Green Harbour.

◆ *WRACKING* ◆

When there were many shipwrecks along the shore, "wracking" was an exciting adventure. Men in little boats went out to salvage cargo that filled their skiffs and sail boats with treasures and supplies that filled their kitchen cupboards. Many of the wrecks provided exotic items: silver spoons and carving sets, wall clocks, plates and dinner sets, chairs and tables. Bolts of "shot taffeta," "Changeable silk" salvaged from the *Hungarian* were made into many a young bride's "pearing out" dress, and fine linen was sewn into babies' christening gowns.

Profiteering became a part of "wracking" when companies took over the business of salvaging cargoes from stranded vessels. When a "half-clear" day was announced, the fishermen who went out to the wreck received half the proceeds from the sale of the goods, or half the goods salvaged. "A fat wreck" was long remembered, but they were few, and as one old man remarked, "Wreck money was only worth a dollar a bushel, Easy come, easy go."

◆

A wreck that provided many lasting memories was the *Bamboro*. Boston bound from Sicily with a cargo of oranges and lemons, she struck the sou'west breakers on the Half Moon in dense fog in April 1894. For miles and miles the tides carried oranges and lemons from her broken hull. Fishermen scooped them up in dip nets; while children ran along the shores collecting the booty, which many of them saw only once a year, in the toe of their Christmas stockings. One man remembered the night she struck the breakers and the boats that came from miles away to fill their holds with oranges and lemons. From Sandy Point came "Captain Al Thorburn and his brother in Captain Al's boat. Father saw them coming and told them it was too late to fill her up that night and come on up to the house. Mother was up at two o'clock in the morning and got breakfast and everybody turned out and helped fill the boat. Come daybreak, all we could see of Captain Al was him goin' around the end of Cape Negro beating it for Shelburne."

"In those days there were plenty of sheep around the shores—hundreds of 'em—and man you talk about eatin' oranges! The lemons they didn't like. They'd get a lemon and bite hard—man alive, they'd screw their jaws around gettin' rid of that lemon. After a time they got so they knew an orange from a lemon, and you could see nothin' but sheep eatin' oranges."

◆ DESERTERS ◆

There are many stories about deserters from warships who came ashore and sought protection. In Sandy Point, three young boys escaped and swam ashore. One of them, Ed Watts, was befriended by a man who hid him in his oatfield and denied having seen him to the seamen searching for the boys. Later, he hid him in his attic, until the ship was gone. Watts spent the remainder of his long life in Sandy Point.

The other boys ran until they reached the banks of the Jordan river, where they were not far ahead of their pursuers. They saw some Indians dipping kiacks near the falls and ran to them. The Micmacs hid them in barrels and covered them with fish until their pursuers had gone on. In Lockeport there are stories of two boys named Capstick and Taylor who escaped from a man o' war; they may have been Watts' companions.

There were two Hardy boys pressed into the British navy in England. They escaped their captors when they reached the port of Boston and were captured and imprisoned. In the old stories, the jailkeeper's daughter fell in love with one of the boys and he with her. One night she unlocked the jail. One went through the woods, and the other, beloved by the girl, was hidden in her house. When soldiers came searching for him she hid him under her wide hooped skirt. They came to Nova Scotia "down Allendale way," and were among the early settlers on the shores of Ragged Islands. Turning to the early records, there was a Joseph Hardy among the early settlers on the shores of Ragged Islands Harbour (Lockeport Harbour), who established himself as a farmer, and eventually received a grant for the two hundred acres where he had laboured.

A story told in Rockland is of a man who, after years at sea, escaped from the man-of-war in which he had been forced to serve. He reached the shores around Port Mouton, and came through the woods to the shores of Ragged Islands Harbour, and changed his name to Frude to hide his identity.

Not far from him came another, David Jeremiah Brown, who had also been pressed into the British navy in England. When he was almost fifteen years old, he went to a pub to get ale for his father and never returned. He had been knocked unconscious by a press gang, and when he awoke he was on a man-o'-war bound for Halifax. He was chosen to be cabin boy and served the captain and officers. He fared very well, but he saw what happened to other young boys, and he deserted and found his way first to Shelburne, then to Lockeport, and later to East Jordan, to a road which became known as Benham's Road for the surname he had chosen, his mother's maiden name.

Another deserter from a British man-o'-war in Shelburne Harbour was William Watt from Manchester, England. According to family lore, when the sailors approached the house where he had taken refuge, an old lady seated in the kitchen churning butter lifted her long skirts and he curled himself on the floor about her feet, with her wide skirts about him. She went on with her churning while the sailors searched her house. When they were gone, young William Watt escaped to Barrington where he became a weaver and married Mary Glance. Their many descendants cherish their family story of the old lady and her wide skirts and their ancestor William Watt.

John Etherington, according to his great-granddaughter, was a native of the parish of Barton and Broat in Yorkshire, when he was taken, at sixteen years of age, by a press gang and put on board the ship *Robust*. He told the captain he would run away if he got a chance. For five years he was held a prisoner until he and another sailor put their clothes on their backs and swam ashore in Cork, Ireland, and boarded a ship bound for America. During the American Revolution he lived in New York. One day when walking along a sidewalk he saw a pretty young woman washing clothes outdoors in the yard. He stopped and asked for a drink of water, became better acquainted and married her. At the end of the war, they came to Shelburne, were given land on McNutt's Island and at Gunning Cove where they lived.

One day he heard a cannon, a signal that a ship was in distress. Unfamiliar with the coast, the captain had tried to push through False Passage, and sent a boat to shore with fifteen men to find where they were. The boat overturned in the breakers and all were lost. When John Etherington went out to the ship, the captain said, "Well, John, you've come back." It was the captain of the *Robust*. Etherington piloted the ship to safe water and was made King's Pilot. He came to Shelburne to live and had a rope walk, a straight path, on Ann Street from the corner of Mowatt to Water Street, where he twisted rope, a skill he had learned in the navy.

Robert Atkinson a native of Dorchester, England, was "captain of the maintop and ship carpenter" when he deserted. One night, when seven young sailors came back late to the ship, it was his duty to flog them or be flogged. He chose to desert. With his ditty bag bound to his shoulders, he jumped overboard, swam ashore, and lay in hiding until the ship left. He went on to Barrington and later settled on Cape Island.

About the same time, John Stoddart deserted a man-o'-war which was accompanying ships bringing Loyalists to Shelburne. He was also a native of England and was a boatswain on the ship. His wife Nancy, who had been with him for three years, was put on shore when they reached Shelburne, and he deserted to be with her. They went by boat to Sherose Island before he purchased an island in Shag Harbour that became know as Stoddard Island.

Conrad Ryer deserted his German regiment that fought with the British during the American Revolution. Having been pressed into the army on his father's farm in Hesse, near Kassel, he deserted in New York and came to Nova Scotia concealed in a barrel. One of his descendants discovered, through research in Germany, that Konrad Ryer had indeed been a soldier and had served in two of the German regiments that came to America. He fought for the British during the American Revolution, and deserted on the September 1, 1783, "leaving his barracks in New York without uniform or arms."

Besides those who came seeking sanctuary in Shelburne County, there were those who were pressed into the British navy by warships that came into Shelburne Harbour, sending press gangs along the shores to pick up helpless young men. Philip Goodick, the son of a Hessian soldier who came to Shelburne following the American Revolution and settled in Sandy Point, was held in the navy for many years, and when Napoleon was rowed ashore as prisoner to the island of St. Helena, he rowed the stroke oar.

Henry Blades served his time in the British navy, and came to Shelburne where he was given a lot of land in the north end of town and one hundred acres on the old Barrington Road. He married Mary Adams and for a time lived in peace in Pubnico. Then, he was pressed into the navy on the frigate *Shannon*, and according to family tradition, he was aboard in June 1813, when the *Chesapeake* was captured by the *Shannon* in Boston Harbour and brought in triumph to Halifax.

♦ *PRIVATEERS* ♦

In stories of the privateers that prowled along the shores of Nova Scotia during the years of the American Revolution and later in the War of 1812, are tales of women who disguised themselves as soldiers, and frightened away the rascals that manned the privateers.

In Shag Harbour, during the War of 1812, a privateer came into the sheltered water of the harbour and dropped anchor. The men were away fishing, and the women gathered together to defend their homes. Hiding behind bushes near the water's edge, they waited until a boat load of freebooters stepped ashore, then a woman with a deep voice shouted, "Fire." The freebooters were soon back on the deck of their privateer.

In Lockeport, where privateersmen had plundered many of their homes and fish houses, and had gone off with their husband's boats, the women were determined to frighten away a boat load of ruffians from coming on shore. Draping red flannel petticoats about their shoulders and hiding behind rocks and trees, their red shoulders well displayed, they made sharp taps on a tub to sound like marching soldiers and fired a musket. The privateers mistook them for redcoats and lost no time in heaving their anchor.

◆ SAILORS AND FISHERMEN ◆

Superstitions shaped from experience are shared among fishermen and sailors as ways that will bring good luck and will dispel bad luck.

To start a day's fishing, a boat must be pushed off stern first and turned clockwise with the sun, for very bad luck will follow a boat turned anti-clockwise, against the sun.

If a crow flies across the bow of a boat when first setting off, bad luck will follow. The boat must be turned back to the wharf and again pushed off stern first and turned with the sun clockwise before taking off to the fishing grounds.

Rope must always be coiled clockwise, and a hatch or bucket must never be turned upside-down for fear the boat will capsize.

In a fisherman's or a sailor's home, cookies and cakes must never be placed upside-down on a plate or eaten "bottom up." A woman of Sandy Point remembered that her father spanked her when she ate a piece of cake upside-down, for he believed his vessel would turn turtle.

In the days of sailing ships, as on boats today, no one must whistle for fear of whistling up a storm.

To buy a little needed wind, throw a penny overboard. A little soft whistling will bring enough wind to fill limp sails.

A knife must never be driven into the hatch on a boat for it will bring bad luck to the boat and those on board.

A bird must never be killed at sea, and a tombstone must never be part of a ship's cargo: disobeying either of these warnings will bring a death.

For good luck, a coin was placed beneath the mast, bringing good luck to the ship and good luck to those who sailed in her; If a fish boat, good luck in fishing.

Some fishermen will not wear anything but white mittens when lobstering.

Socks must have a band of white, otherwise the socks will bring bad luck to the wearer. For good luck, and to bring their loved ones safely home from the sea, women knit a strand of their hair into the web of the socks.

Some colours are not favoured by fishermen. A house or a boat painted blue is bad luck, as is a grey sweater or grey mitts when fishing. The colour pink is also frowned upon by some fishermen for it will bring bad luck to a fish boat.

An all black cat is a "jonah"—very bad luck. Some fishermen will not allow a black cat in their homes. A fisherman, whose mother was given a black kitten by her granddaughter, protested against having a black cat in the house, and killed it after a day of poor fishing.

As black cats are jonahs, women are jonahs and should keep away from fish boats.

Days when fishermen should not go fishing or start a voyage are Fridays, and especially Friday the 13th and March 24th. They should push off on a Saturday or a Sunday.

◆

Putting aside old-fashioned superstitions, a sea captain put off from Sandy Point on a Friday the 13th. When he left port the wind and the sea were a "dead calm." He made the quickest salt-fish trip he ever made and was homeward bound when a gale struck. He latched his schooner down to ride out the gale, and set his mate to watch the long hours of the storm, until nine the next morning when the gale blew out. He weathered the wind of that August twister when many around him went down.

◆

The word "pig" is taboo among fishermen and their families, for the word brings bad luck to fishing and to fish boats. If someone uses any word that refers to this "hoodoo" animal—pig, hog, swine, sow, pork chops, but especially the word pig—some fishermen will not go out in their boats that day. One housewife used to grunt "*oink, oink*" to buy pork or ham at a meat counter; and a pig in a pig pen is referred to as "the queer one." "Have you fed the queer one?" Some refer to a pig as "gruff." On Lockeport vessels it is called a "Dennis" or "Couchou."

◆

There is a story on Cape Sable Island how the word pig became hoodoo. Years ago, a vessel with a cargo of pigs struck a reef offshore near Southside Beach on Cape Island. To lighten their vessel, hoping she would float and release herself from the reef, the pigs were thrown overboard. Their carcasses floated for miles and miles around the shores of the island. One man went out in his little boat and picked up one of the pigs and brought it ashore. The next day when he went out for another pig, he was drowned. The island residents were in a furor. Pigs were hoodoo.

◆

While there are many things that will bring bad luck to fishermen and to fish boats, rollers shaped from dogwood (mountain ash), and thole pins whittled from the same wood—the "witch's tree"—will keep the witches away.

◆

There was an old superstition in the days of sailing ships that a sailor outward bound must never speak of the woods and shores of his homeland. When homeward bound with a fair wind in the sails, they said their wives and sweethearts were towing them on "love's towline."

◆

The old sailing ship days are gone, but not the saying that old sailors never die. They turn into gulls and gannets and fly to Fiddler's Green, where there are lots of pretty girls, and plenty of lime juice and rum.

GLOSSARY

Many words are an expression of the area in which they are used; some are heirlooms, a legacy from a past generation, others are those concerning an occupation. Many of these words appear elsewhere in the text as: "fungy" (Home lore), "barbel" (Sea lore), "pink winks" (Insects and Snakes). Words go beyond boundaries and many of the words in this collection are heard in other communities.

A

Aback, taken: To be stunned by an unexpected event, bad news or an affront, an expressive adaptation of the nautical "aback," sails pressed hard against the mast by a sudden shift in the wind.

Abide: Tolerate, usually used with a negative. "I can't abide that woman and her lofty airs."

Able: Capable, physically strong and intelligent, "an able fisherman." When used with a negative, loss of physical strength is denoted, "He is no longer able to go fishing."

Aboard: An aggressive act, either physical aggression or a strident tongue lashing. "I'll fly aboard o'ye and dance a jig on yer palate." A Cape Island adaptation of "aboard," "to board a ship ... in a hostile manner." (Bowditch, p. 290.)

Ace in the hole: "The fly in the ointment," "the spoke in the wheel," that will prevent achieving an objective.

According to: When young boys went fishing with their fathers, they were paid "according to" the value of their work.

Advertised: When used in the expression "She's been advertised," it refers to a woman who has left her husband and has been "advertised" by him in the local newspaper as having left his bed and board and he is no longer responsible for her debts.

Afterclap: A child born too many months after a husband has gone to war, or to sea, to be his child.

After doing: An idiom expressing that something is in the process of being done. "I'm after doing that right now."

Afterthought: A second child born several years after the first child.

Aggravate: To irritate a wound or sore causing it to swell and fester.

Agricultural ox: Bull.

Ah-da: A term of derision. "Ah-da; just two crusts," said of someone's fruitcake.

Airin' up: Blowing up a storm.

Airy: Windy. "It's airy out today."

All hands: Everyone. "All hands on deck," a call for everyone to get up. "All hands to the wheel," for work to be done; from the nautical. "All hands ahoy!" summoning a ship's company on deck. (Bowditch p. 288.) For a ship that was wrecked on the Coast of Shelburne County, it was written, "She was lost with all hands on board." 2. Odd jobs on a vessel. "In the spring of 1840 ... I shipped again as cook, sailor and All Hands." (*Following the Sea*, p. 15.)

Allow: Admit. Of a proud and active old man, "He won't allow he's three-score years and ten." (*Coast Guard*, May 5, 1955.)

Am: "Am" is sometimes used for "are." A little boy called to his kitten, "Where am you?" On a ship-to-shore phone came a young girl's voice from Cape Island, "I know who you be, but I don't know where you am."

Anent: About, against. "Two landlubber strangers were making disparaging remarks anent the genuine ugliness of Mr. Catfish." (*Coast Guard*, May 15, 1955.)

Anger knot: A wen.

Angel food: Fancy food, pastry and "dressed-up" cakes.

Angora kittens: Rolls of grey dust under a bed.

Ass over kettle. Arse over kettle: To fall from carelessness. "I've gone arse over kettle more'n once. Never hurt me none."

Aunt: A term of endearment for an older woman, used with her Christian name or her Christian and surname, and sometimes with her Christian name and her husband's nickname, as "Aunt Abigail Doddy." (*Down Shore Tales*, p. 66.)

Away: Anywhere beyond Shelburne County. "You'd know to look at him he's from away."

A-window: A sharp-pointed Gothic dormer window, called an "A-window " for its shape. For its sharp sloping wall, it is known as a "head-bumper." It is also called the "widow's peek," the "widow's watch," where many an anxious wife watched for a sail that never returned.

B

Back a letter: Address a letter. Before there were envelopes, letters were written on a sheet of paper, folded and sealed, and the address written on the back of the letter.

Back door, in through the: To be a member or related to a family through an illegitimate relationship.

Back land: The forest land at the back of the wood lots granted to the early settlers.

Backload: All the wood a man could lift and carry on his back from his woodlot to his backyard. There are few today who remember the arduous toil of "backing" wood from the wood lots to burn in cook stoves and base burners.

Back up: Huffy. "She's got her back up about something." Also used to express a slight illness. "He's back up a bit. Not like he used to be."

Backen: 1. To give or take a remedy for a cold. 2. Of the wind, when it changes to the north and then the west.

Bad way: To be sick and ailing.

Baitin' up, icin' up, fuelin' up: Preparing a boat to go fishing; baiting trawl lines, getting ice and fuel on board.

Ball frame: An abacus. In many of the one-room schools, a "ball frame" was an important item used by children to teach themselves to add and subtract by moving the wooden balls along the steel rods.

Barbel: *See* Sea Lore.

Bark, barked: To scrape the skin from the shin bone or the knee. "I barked my knee."

Barrel chair: A homemade chair, usually with rockers, made from a barrel and covered with padding and a slip cover.

Barrens: Dry tracts of land covered with bearberry, scrub spruce and a few hackmatacks, rocks and blueberries, where the land has been burned over for "blueberry barrens." On a clear, chilly September evening it is remembered, "It's a cold night on the barrens tonight."

Batten down: To make a house secure against wind and rain; to put on storm windows and double doors to keep out the cold winds of winter.

Bayman: A vessel designed and built locally in the Allendale-Sable River shipyards for fishing in Bay St. Lawrence.

Be: Sometimes takes the place of "are." In Villagedale a young mother called to her little daughter, "You stay where you be, and I'll come where you're at."

Belabouring: An old word for wife abuse. An old Clarks Harbour merchant remembered, "A man was taken into court for belabouring his wife."

Ben Dodie: A person who lived on Cape Island remembered, "A ben dodie is a 'comglut' (glutton) who never stops eating." Another remembered a "ben dodie" as "a long stick of candy a little boy could buy for a penny." In the memory of older residents of Cape Island, Ben Dodie is remembered as a person who used to appear every spring on the island and lived in a rough shelter. His name was Doty, and when he came to one's house, he was always hungry. As years passed, his name, Ben Dodie has slipped into folk memory as the symbol of a "comglut."

Bible door: A Georgian or Colonial door, a six-panel door, also known as a Christian door, double-Christian door or as a holy door, and called a Bible door because they were laid out as an open bible below the cross.

Birchtown fever: A lazy feeling.

Bloaters: Large plump herring, cured in salt and smoked. In the 1920s they were advertised in the *Coast Guard* as selling in a local Shelburne store for thirty-five cents a dozen.

Blueberry Buckle, Blueberry Fungy: *See* Home Lore.

Blueberry Special: The former Halifax-Southwestern passenger train that puffed its slow way along the south shore from Halifax to Yarmouth.

Bluff of the bow: Where the bow of a boat widens towards the stern. Writing of shipwrecked mariners, "They had kept above the water in what we call 'the bluff of the bow' on floating wreckage in the forecastle." (*Down Shore Tales*, p. 9.)

Bobsleds: Two short sleds fastened one behind the other with a length of chain, used to haul wood from the woodlots. They "bob" over the hummocks and rocks of a rough wood road. "Long sleds" were first used to haul wood. They were too long to go around bends in the wood roads, and were replaced by shorter bobsleds. The runners of the sleds were shod with bands of wood instead of iron. When the wood band became worn they were removed and replaced with new bands of wood.

Boddle: Money or rum passed by a "boodler," one who works for a political party and buys votes. A noted boodler in the Shelburne area was known as "Jimmy the boodler."

Bog trotters: Big, flat feet capable of striding across a bog.

Bold water: Deep water close to the shore. "It was bold water right up to the wooded shores, and we ran in close and hauled aback the yards within a mile of the land." (*Following the Sea*, p. 85.)

Boned: To enquire with curiosity. "I boned him hard to find out if he had a girlfriend."

Born in a fishing boat: Boats were manned by local skippers, "who we might say ... 'were born in a fishing boat.'" (*Down Shore Tales*, p. 29.)

Boston bucket: "Down Blanche way a man caught a codfish with a head on it as big as a Boston bucket."

Box boat: *See* Pram.

Boxing Rock: A large, flat-topped rock off the shore at Hart's Point, exposed at low tide. In an old story, the rock was given its name from an incident in Shelburne's early history. On one of the vessels that came into the harbour were two young men who fought each other. The captain, seeing the large flat rock standing above the waves, set the two on the rock and told them to do their boxing there.

Boy: The young fellow who goes in a fish or lobster boat as a helping hand. Later he will be a "hired man." "I've been fishing all my life, man and boy." "Boy" is also used as an expletive: "They found a petrified woman one time—just solid stone, boy." (*Voice of the Pioneer*, "Those waters off (Cape) Sable Island," p. 75.)

Brine in their veins: "The sea still pulls at those who have its brine in their veins" (Evelyn Richardson, "Cruise of the Ocean Belle," *Dalhousie Review*, Vol XXIX No. 1, p.7.)

Browse: Green salad.

Buck wood: To saw wood with a bucksaw: one who "bucked wood" for a living was known as Sawbuck Jim.

Buckle a cod: A response to a good fish yarn—"Wouldn't that buckle a cod."

Buckle to: To work hard to make both ends meet. Of one woman it was said, "She buckled to and made a living for her children weaving rag rugs." Some fail to make a good living because they cannot "buckle down."

Bucko mates: A rough domineering bully. "Yarmouth ships sailed to all parts on the globe and the reputation of some 'bucko' mates was not of the best." (*Down Shore Tales*, p. 69.)

Buds: The red berries of the wild rose. Strung into long loops of berries they were used to decorate Christmas trees.

Bunch: A hummock of moss and fern roots. A man reported he fell "over a bunch and split my knee," when backing wood from his woodlot.

Bundle: Large sum of money. "Why doesn't he stop working? He's made his bundle."

Butter tub: "Didn't she set herself in a butter tub," said of a young girl who married a wealthy young man.

Button the door: A wooden bar device turned crosswise over the door secures it against intruders. Before going to bed, remember, "turn the button on the door."

C

Cabbage: To commandeer; to get someone to work without pay. "She'll cabbage some little fella to do her digging."

Cadiddles: Odds and ends of food that can be used for a "leftover" supper.

Caesar's Pond: A boggy pond lying well to the southeast of Barrington. In an old story, a man and his ox named Caesar were in the woods and Caesar walked into the pond and was dragged down into the deep muck.

Cant hook: A long-handled, adjustable iron hook used by a stonemason to move foundation stones, first moving the rock to a certain cant and holding it with the hook. The same hook was also used in rolling logs.

Caplog: The log or timber around the edge of a wharf or boat landing; a curbing. *Also* String piece.

Cape Island boat: *See* Sea Lore.

Cape Island sneakers: Hip rubber boots worn by fisherman.

Captain's watch: The railed platform on the roof of a house reached by a ladder from the attic floor. It also shares with an A-window the name "widow's watch" where many an anxious wife watched for a sail to return.

Cart wheel: A large, one-inch copper coin which was worth a cent or a penny. It was used to trace circles on a piece of woolen cloth, to be cut from the cloth and feather-stitched to squares of flannel pieced together for a "coinmat." "Cart wheels" were also known as "coppers." "When kids we worked all day for a copper."

Catch a kink: A fisherman's expression for a short nap.

Catching a crab: When a rower misses a stroke and is thrown forward to the bottom of a boat, he is said to be "catching a crab."

Chamber: The upper floor of a house was known as the "chamber." When divided into rooms for sleeping, each room was called a chamber. Sometimes the word was applied only to an unfinished portion of the floor used for storage, or a "rough room."

Changeable silk: Cloth woven of two strands of contrasting colours which reflect changing hues as the light accents the colours of the woof or the warp. When the cloth is taffeta it is called "shot taffeta."

Chick nor child: If one has neither "chick nor child," one is poor indeed.

Chimley: Chimney. "That's the way we used to say it for chimney."

Chimney lice: The tiny sparks that catch in the soot at the back of a fireplace and creep around in the soot. Another name for "chimney lice," is "red soldiers." When they move in the soot, "The soldiers (or red coats) are marching."

Christian door: *See* Bible door.

Christmas tree: A bright triangular fish lure made by fishermen from aluminum with thin, silvered spinners and two white feathers to attract pollock and cod.

Chuck, chucked: Expressive words of motion. "I've got a stove that sure chucks the heat." For the wind: "It chucked around in the night from the sou'east to the sou'west and there it stuck."

Circle: A group of women working together, as a sewing circle, to raise money for a church or community project.

Clabboards: Clapboards, weather boards. The narrow boards used for covering houses, in older houses their ends were often bevelled and lapped, rather than butted.

Clammer: One who digs clams, to sell to fishermen for ground bait considered the best bait to catch ground fish.

Claydee: A small white claypipe. A woman remembers her grandfather used to call to her, "Bring me my old claydee." When her grandfather was out of sight, she used to blow bubbles with his old "claydee." A C.D. was a claypipe "aged grandmothers used to enjoy." (*Down Shore Tales*, p. 41.)

Clever: Hospitable. One in Blanche told a young man "Your old grandmother was a clever woman. When you went to her door she put the kettle on for a pot of tea."

Clipping: Moving at a rapid speed, as in a boat, "Clipping it at 12 knots." (*Coast Guard*, June 25, 1965.)

Clock feather: A hen's feather used to oil a clock.

Clod hoppers: Heavy boots, broad and thick, soled for "clod hopping."

Cobbing: A beating, a *walloping*. From "cob," an old sailor's term for a beating on the breeches with a flat piece of wood.

Cockerwit: From "Coqiwit," the Micmac name for Woods Harbour as recorded in 1772 in the confirmation of a grant of 1000 acres of land to Rev. Samuel Wood "called by the Indians Coqiwit, now called Woods Harbour." An old Indian remembered that *coqueit* was the Micmac name of the old squaw, the long-tailed duck, that calls *cock-a-link, cock-a-link, cock-a-link.*

Cockerwitter: A native of Cockerwit. (Woods Harbour.)

Cockled: Perched precariously as a boat "cockled atop an iceheap." (Evelyn Richardson, "Cruise of the Ocean Belle," *Dalhousie Review,* XXIX No. 1 p. 7.)

Cockles: Species of lichen. *See* Plant Lore. Also called crockers.

Codding: kidding, "You're codding me."

Codger: To put together a meal from odds and ends. "I gotta codger up something for supper." (*Villagedale.*)

Codseeker: A fishing vessel designed and built to "seek" and catch cod.

Come: Used as an expletive. "Come a lur'd day. Freddie will fix the fence."

Comglut: A glutten. *See* Ben Dodie.

Commons: Used in Blanche when expressing doubt about a lack of good manners. "I guess you'll say we have no commons."

Cookie: A young boy on a fish boat who helps the cook. "He's a smart cookie," refers not to a young boy on a fish boat, but to a man who can deceive others.

Corker: A very severe tempest with heavy wind and rain.

Crack: To work vigorously. "They do a crack of work in no time short." To move on. "When they hear there is no beer they shake their heads and crack on." (*Coast Guard,* June 6, 1989.)

Crack, cried: Noisy protest. "When we put the little fella to bed, he was so tired he never cried crack."

Crackleware: Pottery with a cracked glaze.

Cranks: Physical disabilities. "Lou and his cranks."

Cream and molasses: A mulatto. "Some nowadays are more cream than molasses."

Cre'sut: Creosote. The thick black soot that clings to stove covers and the brick walls of fireplaces. When the "wild geese" and "soldiers" (sparks caught in the creosote) march in the "sut" there will be rain. As an old home remedy it was used to "backen" a toothache.

Crick: Creek. Along the shores a "crick" is a narrow inlet filled with water at high tide, drained with the ebb tide. In Newellton to go "round the crick" is to go over the crick towards Centreville, a term that perhaps stems from the days before there was a bridge over the creek and to reach the other side one had to walk around.

Cricket: A wooden footstool.

Cripple Crick: A creek through the marsh on the south side of Cape Island. There are stories how it was named "Cripple Crick." In the days when Cripple Creek became famous during the Colorado goldrush, a mail driver noticed that the men working on the road beside the creek were crippled. He told the eager young men who wanted to go to Colorado, "Here is Cripple Crick." Another story is of crippled birds that seek shelter in the creek.

Crocus bag: Coarse burlap bag used for oats or middlings.

Croodled: To hide, "Well I croodled down in the grass and I says 'Go right away—this is no place for wimmen'." (*Down Shore Tales,* p. 27.)

Cross fox: *See* Patch fox.

Crotch: A fork in a channel. "The crotch of the channel made a sharp turn to the right." (*Coast Guard*, February 25, 1933 p.6.)

Crow's nest: A method of criss-crossing firewood at the ends of the rows as the wood is piled to prevent bulging and the wood falling to the floor.

Crumber: A brush and tray used to brush crumbs from a tablecloth.

Cryolite: An old name in Barrington for milkglass, perhaps for its shining lustre like the cryolite brought from Greenland.

Cubby hole: A small closet, especially one under a staircase.

Cud, cuddy: A cabin at the bow of a small undecked boat or vessel, used for storage of provisions and equipped with bunks and cookstove.

Cut stick: To move quickly. "The whales that we see generally do cut stick so quick that we could not hitch to another." (Captain James Doane Coffin, *Journal of the Margaret Rait*, p.48.)

D

Dabby: Skimpy. A dabby dress is too short and tight, and of thin material.

Dancing beggars: A waggish epithet bestowed upon the Shelburne Loyalists for their love of dancing, by one of the early merchants, reported to have been William Hargraves.

Deadfall: A pit dug in a path or across a moose or deer trail, covered with debris, into which an animal falling could not regain the path and fell prey to hunters. An old deadfall in Coffinscroft was still visible in the early 1900s. Also called "pitfalls."

Dead horse: To pay for something already used is to pay for a "dead horse."

Deadman: A prop placed against a tree and wedged into the ground to prevent a tree from falling in the wrong direction.

Dead off: In a straight direction. "There's Green Island dead off Little Port L'Hebert."

Dead soldier: A discarded beer bottle.

Dear: As an expletive, "dear" denotes a friendly feeling and may be used between strangers. On asking the way to the lighthouse, an old man said to a visitor, "Well, dear, walk down this road a piece and turn left."

GLOSSARY

Death roll: In early editions of the *Coast Guard*, the obituary column.

Decess: An old word used in Ingomar for a "jonah," one who never succeeds. Perhaps derived from "decession," to decrease.

Deep baseboard: Wainscot. In many of the older houses a wainscot "sealed" the lower walls of a room. Some were of wide boards, "squareboarded," placed horizontally as vessels were built of planks; others were of upright staves, barrel staves and were known as "staving." A chair rail, a molding cut from wood, topped the staving to prevent chairs from bruising the staving. A chair rail was also used on a plastered wall, "But," said one woman, "I took mine down 'cus it ketched the dirt."

Dennis: A name for a pig on a fishing vessel. *See* Sea Lore.

Devil: There are many devils lurking in the offing: "the devil's at your elbow" when you have good luck at cards; "it's the devil's own luck" to make port or to achieve success without careful planning. When "there's devil a one," there's nothing left over; and in an empty bottle "there's devil a drop." When something is left over "the devil take the hindmost;" and, fear not, "the devil looks after his own."

Diagonal rage: Someone on Cape Island was said to have been so mad he had a diagonal rage.

Dick Alldry: An old nickname for an alcoholic. A certain Dick Alldry "who lived to the easterd of Lockeport" is remembered for saying of his former employer's wife, "She takes nothin' from nothin' and nothin' remains."

Die sly: To die suddenly and unexpectedly. "Didn't she die sly!"

Digging up hoe: The symbol of a resourceful people—the New England fishermen and boat builders "who settled this coast and with little more than their two hands and a 'digging up hoe' made homes along the rocky shore and wrestled a living from the treacherous sea and a reluctant soil." (Evelyn

215

Richardson, "The Old Chairmaker." *Dalhousie Review,* April 1947.)

Ding-a-ma-doggy: A "ding-a-ma-doggy" in the Shelburne schoolyard is the same as a "thing-a-ma-jig" or a "thing-a-ma-jiggy" which may be used to refer to anything, especially if the name is unknown. "Pass me the ding-a-ma-doggy."

Dinging: A beating, perhaps from the old Scottish word "ding" "to thrust or dash with violence." (*Webster's Dictionary,* 1904.)

Dinner-bah: Mid-morning break for a cup of tea. *See* Home Lore.

Dinner tub: A large wooden container used to hold enough food for a week when out fishing.

Ditty box, ditty bag: *See* Sea Lore.

Divvy: To divide into portions, as food or clothing.

Dixon's dog: A dog that barks and guides a skipper to safe anchorage. "They said some of our old time skippers used to locate their position either by catching a fish when they would decide by its appearance just what shoal it was on, or that they would hear the barking of `Dixon's Dog' as they came nearer the coast, and govern themselves accordingly." *(Down Shore Tales,* p. 32.)

Doflicker: Used to designate someone whose surname cannot be recalled, "Mrs. Doflicker across the way." The word is also used to refer to an object, of which the name is forgotten.

Dog house: In Lockeport a small room in a fish plant with benches around the wall where the workers eat their meals from their dinner pails.

Dog traders: The expression "Our grandfathers traded dogs," referred to distant blood relations. The dog traders were more closely related than, say, 42nd cousins.

Doless: A person with little inclination to work.

Dollard: A two-arm cleat on a wharf to hold a rope from a ship.

Dolly: A small four-wheeled pushcart used in the woodlots to transport short pieces of wood, and around farms and in the backyards of houses.

Dolphins: Fixed bouys to mark safe passage through sand and mud flats to deep water.

Door stool: The threshold of a front or back door, perhaps adapted from the shipbuilders' term for a firm foundation for machinery on board a vessel.

Double-bitted: An axe with two sharp cutting edges.

Double house: Two houses joined together, usually built by two brothers sharing the same property.

Down east: To homesick Nova Scotians who had sought work in the New England States, Nova Scotia was "down east."

Down easter: In the New England States, a ship or a sailor from Nova Scotia.

Down shore: "Down shore" is to the east; "up the shore," to the west.

Drawn: Boiled or melted to draw the flavour, as for drawn butter sauce.

Drake's drums: The beat of the surf against the shore. "The Atlantic rollers boom like Drake's drums." (*Coast Guard*, May 5, 1955.)

Drank the King's money: In stories of impressment into the King's navy, there were those who drank the King's money. A friendly stranger offered a young man in a tavern a mug of grog in which he dropped a coin, a shilling. When the mug was empty, he was told by the friendly stranger, "You are now in the King's navy. You drank the King's money."

Dreen: A drain that draws water from the land. In the expression, "He dreened me," an opponent in a game of 45s has played a high trump card and draws the five of trumps from the bidder's hand.

Drokes: Stumps of old trees in bogs and on the barrens.

Drop: Write. "I will drop her a line later." "I must drop another word or two," wrote a diarist of Little Harbour in the 1890s as she began to write in her diary.

Droppies: Dust swept into piles when sweeping.

Dry-handed: Uppish. Those who do "dry-handed work," paper work, are suspected by those who fish, or labour with their hands, to be uppish.

Dubber: An adze.

Duck tub: A tub or barrel made into a float in which a duck hunter hides. The tub floats in among the ducks. Also a "gunning tub."

Dude stick: A fancy cane. "Who's that fop flippin' his little dude stick?"

Dumb fish: The darker grades of dry fish; spoiled salt fish.

Dumbdora: A stupid young girl; pretty, but stupid.

Dusting: To move quickly. A little boy of Welshtown told a friend, "I gave my cat a ball and when she see it what dusting it over the floor."

E

Ears: Handles on dishes, cups, pitchers, and jugs. "I've got a butter dish nigh as deep as this, but it h'aint got ears on it like this."

Elbow: A point of land." Past the elbow of the Cape (Cape Sable), westward is the Bay."

Empt: Empty.

Eyebrow windows: The small windows beneath the eaves, fairly common in houses in the Barrington area. *Also* called prayer windows.

Eye seed: A flax seed used to remove dirt from beneath an eyelid.

Eye winkers: Eyelashes.

F

Fagged out: The frayed edges of garments or cloth, in sailors' parlance, "fag end" for a frayed rope end. A person can be fagged out, exhausted from heavy labour.

Family way: Pregnant

Fancy work: Fine needlework, embroidery; fine fretwork cut from wood with a fretsaw and applied as trimming to a house.

Farmed out: To place or give a child to a friend or relative to care for. "In the old days many a widow left penniless farmed out a child to a friend to care for."

Favour the tide: To sail with the direction of the tide.

Favours: Resembles. "Her young one sure favours the old man, and he's the splitting image of his old man. Joany, now, favours the other side of the house."

Feelers: Antenna-like appendages attached to the head of moths and butterflies and some insects.

Fetch, fetched: 1. With its strong nautical flavour, "fetch" is used to raise, as a boat, "to fetch it up." 2. To reach a destination; "Let her come around and we'll stand off shore … then tack, and I think we'll fetch up by Bantam." (*Down Shore Tales*, p. 32.) An old fisherman remembered that his boat fetched up against a reef. 3. To bring, as a baby. "Old granny Hannah (a midwife) fetched many a baby." For a door that sagged, an old woman thought her house "swayed and fetched it up." 4. Then one can always fetch a hoot and get things going.

Fever glass: A thermometer.

Fig of tobacco: A plug of tobacco. Chewing tobacco pressed into thin layers or blocks ready to be cut into "cuds" to be chewed.

File Bottom: A vessel designed and built with a sharp bow for fast sculling. *See* Sharp Shooter.

Finish kind: The very best of anything.

First comers: The New Englanders, the first English-speaking settlers who came mainly from Cape Cod, of whom many were descendants of the Pilgrim Fathers who came to America on the *Mayflower*.

Fish killer: A "highline" fisherman, one who catches the most fish. "Captain 'Jack' used to tell of the renowned fish killer, Captain 'Sol' Jacobs bringing his fare of several hundred barrels of mackerel and paying him in $10 and $20 gold pieces which he dropped down into his rubber boots, the weight being such that he had a hard job to climb up over the beach at John's Island." (*Down Shore Tales,* p. 30.)

Fish man: The man who comes to the door with fresh fish for sale.

Fish yarn: A fish tale, to be taken with a grain of salt.

Fished: To haul or lift up from the water. "Roy rushed to the scene and jumping in, grabbed the little girl and held her until her brother arrived and fished them both from the water."(*Coast Guard,* March 12, 1931).

Fixing: Planning, arranging. "I'm fixing on goin' home come spring."

Flat calm: Completely still, dead calm.

Flat footed: A negative vote. "The *Hants Journal* last week flat footed an open season for moose." (*Coast Guard,* March 31, 1931).

Flying axehandles: Diarrhoea.

Flying jib: Get things moving in a hurry. "Put the flying jib to that milk pitcher."

Foggies: A Clarks Harbour baseball team in the 1930s.

Follow the sea: To go to sea, to follow it as a profession. One mother proudly remembered, "My son followed the sea all his life."

Forelay: To prepare for the future.

Former: A smooth, flat piece of wood used as a gauge when knitting fish nets and pot heads for lobster traps for a uniform mesh.

Forty winks: A short nap in the daytime.

Free nigger: An expression used when hard labour is finished and one is free from work. The expression perhaps came into use following the arrival of the Freed Blacks sent to Shelburne following the American Revolution and settled in Birchtown at the head of Birchtown Bay. (*King's Bounty*. The Freed Blacks. pp. 83-106.)

Freshen: 1. A dull wind that stirs into a fresh breeze. "Early Sunday night the wind began to freshen from the south and the craft at the wreck found shelter at the Tusket Islands. Next morning was a howling gale from the south." (*Down Shore Tales*, p. 42.) 2. When a cow gives birth to a calf, she freshens.

Frog droll: The green scum on stagnant water in ditches and shallow ponds.

Front room: The parlour at the front of the house.

Funnel: A stove-pipe.

G

Gaft: A gaff, an iron hook attached to a short wooden handle used on a fish boat to haul or lift objects from the water.

Gaffed: Lifted or hauled with a gaff. "Andrew gaffed a buoy, hauled up the trap and filled it to the top with lobsters." (*Down Shore Tales*, p. 35.)

Gannet neck: A person with a long neck like a gannet.

Gansey frock: A clergyman's fine black gown.

Gap and swallow: Soup. "It's time for gap and swallow."

Garget milk: The milk from a cow's udder when she is "drying off" before she freshens.

Geely crawley, geely crailey, geeny criny, geeny crilaly: "Well, geely! Old son." Lively expressions from Cape Sable Island.

Gentleman: A polite name for a bull.

Gimp: Energy, vim. One who has no "gimp" is lackadaisical, has no "get up and go."

Girl, the: A man's wife. "My father always called my mother 'the girl.'"

Glory hole: A cupboard, usually one under the stairs filled with odds and ends. In old nautical terms on a tramp steamer, the forecastle.

Go-devil: A long light wood sled with the ends of the runners curved inward to facilitate passing through narrow wood roads. It glided swiftly over the snow giving the expression. "Go like a go-devil."

Going to meeting clothes: One's best clothes put aside for going to church.

Goin' groggen': Off on a drunken spree.

Gooseberry: When two is company and three a crowd, the third person is a gooseberry.

Goosenest: Grey feathers of dust under a bed.

Granny: A midwife.

Greased lightning: To move very quickly. A little boy boasted, "I had a dog once could go faster than greased lightning."

Green fish: Fish split and salted but not dried.

Grew on a tree: Someone of doubtful parentage. "I guess he must have grew on a tree."

Groaner: A fog horn that utters deep groans of warning.

Grouty: of a mean disposition.

Ground swell: A strange swelling of the ocean near the shore that lifts a small boat and swings it to port or starboard. A ground swell lies off Point Carleton (Fort Point), near the western shores of Shelburne Harbour.

Grub pail: A fisherman's term for the food taken on board a boat outward bound to the fishing grounds, taken on board in a pail or in a wooden tub. *See* Dinner tub.

Gull's bait: A half-sick feeling when one is not "up to scratch," not even good for gull's bait.

Gulls and gannets: The souls of old sailors. *See* Sealore.

Gully hole: The depression at the collar bone. A prime target in days of home remedies for application of remedies to "backen" a cold.

Gunning tub: *See* Duck tub.

Gurry: Fish offal; waste from cleaning fish.

Guzzle: A shallow pool of water left on the sand flats at ebb tide. Also a shallow inlet of water in a marsh where seabirds congregate giving to the inlet the name "duck guzzle."

H

H'aint: An expressive negative. "H'aint not" and "H'aint so" overheard in an argument in Woods Harbour. "It'll be cold this spring. H'aint not had winter."

Half-baked, half there: A simpleton.

Half cut: Slightly intoxicated; "whole cut," dead drunk.

Half house: Half a Cape Cod house, with the front entrance to the house at one side of the front of the house with two windows to the right or left of the door. By adding to the house to the right or left of the door, it became a full Cape Cod with the door in the centre and windows on each side.

Half Moons, Half Moon: Local names for the Salvages lying to the south of Cape Negro Harbour. In local traditions, when the lighthouse was built on the Salvages, from Port La Tour in a shimmering light it looked like a half moon.

Hand-barrow: The two poles used to carry hay stacks from the hay field to the barn. With slats across the poles they were used to "hand-barrow" fish from the shore to the fish house. Before there was a horse-drawn hearse, a hand-barrow was used to carry the coffin to the grave for burial.

Handling: To transport fish from place to place. "He doesn't go fishing — he just uses his boat for handling."

Handy boy: A young boy who works as a helping hand on a fish boat. "In her, Captain Doane's young sons—sailed as crewmen and handy boys, catching their first cod and digging and shucking clams for bait." (*Annals of a Barrington Shipyard,* p. 130.)

Hard fisherman: A fisherman who goes off fishing in all kinds of weather.

Hard money: An old name for coins.

Hard sledding: To labour very hard to make "both ends meet."

Haul: As a nautical term, "haul" is a well-used and expressive word. For fine weather, the wind must haul through the south into the west. Oxen haul, never pull. A good catch of lobsters is a good haul. "He come in with a pretty good haul of lobsters." (*Voice of the Pioneer,* p. 76.) Boats are hauled up the skids to dry land.

Haul-over: A narrow canal cut across the isthmus of Cape Negro Harbour to the shores of Port La Tour Harbour to haul small boats from one harbour to the other. It was first cut across the land in the 1820s and later was widened to accommodate larger fish boats. (*Coast Guard,* June 13, 1963, "History and Folklore of Shelburne County," No. 14.)

He and she: Some things are he; some things are she. A lobster is "he"; fog is "she." A boat is "she," as is a wreck. "I mind well the day she came ashore. The fog, she was thick as soup." With pride, a Cape Island fisherman looked at his Cape Islander, "She's the perfect boat." (*Voice of the Pioneer,* p. 72.)

Head bumper: *See* A-Window.

Hebeegeebees: An attack of upset nerves. "With her tongue, she'll give anyone the hebeegeebees."

Heel spoon: A shoe horn.

Hef, heft: Weight, full force. Of a storm at sea a young man of Sandy Point boasted that he stayed fishing on Quero when others fled a brewing gale, but "we didn't get the heft of it even on Quero." An old lady of Newellton said of her cane, "It takes the hef' off my leg."

Hellish slow and wobbly; hellish slow workings: Nicknames, HSW, for the old Halifax and Southwestern train that swayed and wobbled over a poor rail bed and around curves, and was seldom on time.

Hen's nests: Swirls of dry hay left in a hay field.

Hen scratches: Fine wrinkles spreading outward from the corner of the eyes.

Herrin' choker: A native born Nova Scotian.

Herring scale: the old five-cent silver coin, "the size of a herring scale, or thereabouts."

Highfalutin: High-blown opinions, especially an oversized opinion of one's own merits.

High-stepper: A young man over fond of the girls; a young woman mincing around on high heels. "Look at that high-stepper mincing around on egg shells."

Hind-side-fore, hind-side-to: A garment put on "wrong side out" or inside-out.

Hind-most: Whatever is left over. "The devil take the hindmost."

Hip: To walk with a bounce.

Hip waders: A fisherman's hip-high rubber boots.

Hit: To ask a favour. "She hit me up to take her home."

Hitch: A short visit. "I saw her when I was down there a hitch or two ago."

Hi-yi: In Lockeport, "hi-yi" is a lively expression. It is used as a greeting, as an expression of surprise or pleasure, as a compliment. "Hi-yi, you! Will you look at that." "Getting your wood in today. Hi-yi, sticky." "Ya doin' a good job, hi-yi sticky."

Holder: Pieces of cloth cut in a square and padded to protect the hands when handling hot dishes.

Holiday: A portion of woodwork overlooked by the painter.

Holy: As a mild expletive, "holy" is a lively word. Holy mackerel, holy old mackinaw, holy mister man, holy red smoke, holy jees. "All the boats were comin in, and holy jees, no sign of the old man." (*The Lockeport Lockout*, p. 1.)

Hospital: Using the meaning of "hospital" as a place for shelter, come two placenames in Shelburne County: Hospital Cove, the landlocked inlet lying between Sherose Island and the opposite shore at Crowells, and Hospital Passage, the passage of water west of Clarks Harbour between the islands of Seal and Mud.

House, The other side of the: The maternal side of the family. "He gets his good looks from the other side of the house. His father is as homely as all outdoors."

Hove: A nautical term in origin, "hove" is used on shore and at sea. 1. To heave, to throw: "He hove the bottle on shore." 2. To appear: "She hove in sight swaying like a square-rigger." 3. To stop or tarry: "They come up the road and hove to." "They've hove to for the summer like summer people."

Humdinger: Large, intense; a humdinger of a watermelon, or a humdinger of a thunderstorm.

Hunkydory: A flat stick of sugar candy a little boy could buy, less than a century ago, for a penny. The word has been extended to refer, perhaps because of the candy, to everything that's grand.

Hurrah's nest: A cluttered, untidy room.

Husher: A crocheted cover for the lid of a chamber pot.

I

Ice: For ice there are a number of combinations to express its appearance. "Ice cakes," mounds of broken ice stranded on a marsh or along the shore or floating on the tide; "ice rafts" and "ice pans," piles of floating ice cakes; "growling ice," ice that growls as the pans of ice grate together and break. "Shell ice," a light "skim of ice;" "black ice," a "skim of ice" covering a black pavement; "ice jam," ice packed as a dam against a flow of water. In Shelburne, "ice weather" is the cold of late spring when the icebergs are drifting off the Cape Breton coast.

Icelanders: Settlers from Iceland who came to Lockeport in 1878. Of those who came, only the Huskilson family remained as permanent settlers.

Idler: This word used by fishermen on vessels employed in the handline fisheries, described one who served the "throaters" and the "splitters." (*Down Shore Tales,* p. 68.) It is an adaptation of the nautical term for those who do constant day duty on board ship and never a night watch.

Imagine: To fancy; to guess. "Imagine that." "I imagine I'll go." "I imagine you're right."

Indian meal: Cornmeal.

In kind: To pay in kind is to pay debts with the products of one's labour, as a woodsman with wood, to a fisherman for fish.

Interesting condition: A way of speaking of a pregnancy.

Isinglass: A local name for mica, thin, transparent sheets inserted in the framework of stove doors especially in the old base burners.

J

Jack donkey: A sailor who hauled a "donkey," a cart fitted with a tongue and crossbar to haul by hand. To reballast a ship, "each jacktar was transformed from a sailor to a Jack donkey, hauling ballast rocks and stowing them on board." (*Following the Sea*, p. 197.)

Jag: A mild drinking spree.

Jowls: The clamps connecting a bit and brace.

Jeeley crawley: "Well jeeley crawley!" "Well Jenney Criney!" Expressions sometimes shortened to, "Well Jeeley! Well Cheese Whiz! *See* Geeley crawley.

Jezebel: A young lady of questionable character.

Jib: A small portion of land, food or cloth. Jiblet: A very small portion of land, food, cloth, or anything not generous in size.

Jigger: Any small boat such as a pinkie, equipped with gear to jig fish, "He had learnt his trade on Gloucester vessels, the mackerel "jiggers" off the Nova Scotian coast." (Evelyn Richardson. "The Cruise of the *Ocean Belle*", *Dalhousie Review, Vol XXIX*, No.1, p. 1.)

Jingler: A chamber pot.

Joe Bluff: To put on a big front to deceive one's opponents in a card game.

Johnny-come-late: A child born several years after the other children in a family.

Jowl: The cheek and jaw bone, of a pig used to make head cheese.

Junk: A short piece of wood.

K

Kaplunk: To come down, to fall down, with a hard bump.

Keel over: To fall over from exhaustion.

Keeler: A wooden disk like a basin, first made by the Indians from a log scooped into shape with a crooked knife. Sometimes the Indians took a hollow log, smoothed it inside, put a bottom to the log cut to the desired height, level around the top, leaving a portion of the rim uncut and shaped it for a handle. Some of the older people in the 1930s called a keeler, a "keelin."

Keen: 1. Sharp-witted. 2. Cold and frosty, of the weather.

Keg, kag: A small barrel used as a float or buoy for a fish net. Also used as a container for nails and other hardware. One fisherman of Cape Island remembered, "In the old rum-running days, we used to pick up the odd keg of rum or whiskey that washed off the decks of a rum-runner." (*Voice of the Pioneer*, p. 74.)

Ketch: Catch. "The door to my house used to ketch up tight."

Kilter skilter: Everything out of order in disarray. *Also,* hilter skilter.

Kinda: Kind of. "I get kinda lonesome for all that today, when you see the boats go out and you don't go." (*Voice of the Pioneer,* p. 75.)

Knit: To tie knots in twine in open meshes with a flat netting needle, for fish nets and pot heads in lobster traps.

Knee windows: *See* Eyebrow windows.

Knockabouts: Old tattered shoes worn about the house or in a fishboat.

Knock down: An introduction.

Knuckle down: To settle down to hard work.

L

Labouring oar: A husband who helps with the housework. "I'm her labouring oar. I do all the work around here."

Labradorman: A vessel designed and built to fish for cod along the coast of Labrador during the summer months, especially those built in Allendale in the late 1800s. (*Coast Guard,* March 12, 1933.)

Lady's chair: A rocking chair with low arms in which a mother can sit and nurse her baby.

Lambast: To beat or to chide roughly.

Lanch: To launch a vessel from the ways, down the skids into the water.

Land of Cakes: An old name on Cape Island for Barrington where they made their cakes of fine white sugar; on Cape Island they made cakes with molasses. The name goes back to at least the 1840s when Captain James Doane Coffin of Barrington wrote in his whaling journal, of some political punning written by Tom Tickle 'em in the *Acadian Recorder*: "So that if I ever see the land of cakes again I may find some more of Tom's quibbling." (*Journal of Margaret Rait,* p. 59.)

Land sharks: Those who go out from the land to pick the ribs of a wreck, and fill little boats with treasures from her broken hull.

Lab-board, lap-work construction: Local boatbuilders' term for a clinker-built vessel with the exterior planks overlapping each other.

Larrigans: Heavy lumbermen's boots worn in the woods when lumbering.

Lay over: To remain in port for a period of time. "The next Saturday night they arrived in Clarks Harbour along with the rest of the fleet to lay over Sunday." (*Down Shore Tales*, p.43.)

Lazy bed: *See* Ol' pogies.

Lazy man's load: More than should be carried in one load, to save having to return for a second load.

Lead line: A sounding line. *See* Sea Lore.

Leading line: A line attached from one vessel or boat to another vessel, to a mooring or to a wharf. "The staysail halyards were unwoven and used as a leading line to the boat which was at once manned by the mate and two seamen ... after the first men landed, the boat was pulled back again and the remaining members of the crew were landed safely." (*Coast Guard*, September 8, 1955.)

Leading wind: A fair wind favourable to a ship's course that will carry a vessel to her destination. "The narrow passage inside Ram Island should never be attempted by strangers ... but vessels from the eastward with a leading wind can pass between Emulous and Farm Ledges." (*Nova Scotia Pilot*, p.12.)

Leaked: Urinate. "A dog leaked on my pansies ... burned 'em right off."

Lean: A wooden prop. A little boy offered, "I'll make you a lean" to keep an apple tree from leaning toward the ground.

Leather the sails: To stitch leather on the sails to prevent chafing.

Leery: Suspicious. A leery person is one not to be trusted.

Left us: A way of speaking of death in memorials in local papers. "In loving memory of—who left us suddenly in March—." "Went away" and "went to be with the Lord" are other ways of expressing the "passing" of a friend or relative.

Lick-ah-de-split, lick-ah-de-cut: To run very fast. "The last I saw of her she was goin' it lick-ah-de-cut."

Licked: To lose a game to an opponent. "He licked me at 45s."

Licking: A whipping.

Lift: A ride. "She hit me up for a lift home."

Likeness: A photo. An old lady remembered, "He invented something—real bright he was—had his likeness in the papers more than once."

Line gale: The high winds that come in March and in September when the sun crosses the "line" (equator).

Ling-toe, ling-toe: A way of walking across wet and boggy land. A woman who grew up in Newellton in the 1880s remembered a man who lived on the southern side of Cape Island coming to their house to visit her father. Her father asked, "How did you come?" His friend replied, "Well, it was this way, Freddie. I came ling-toe, ling-toe' cross South side vannah."

Linking in: Repairing a scallop rake by weaving or looping in the "rope backs" on a scallop rake that has been damaged during dragging operations. (*Coast Guard*, May 31, 1963.)

Little Cod: A small cast iron stove used in the cuddy of a fish boat.

List: The finely woven edge, or selvage, of cloth which was used as garters for men, and was tacked around doors as weather stripping.

Liver pins: In an old belief, the liver was held in place by liver pins. A sudden jolt displacing the pins was a serious mishap, causing the liver to protrude.

Living gale: A violent wind storm. "A living gale sprang up from the south-east, and by midnight, Mike Wrayton, lashed to the wheel in an 80-mile gale, feared, for the first time during all the misfortunes of the voyage, that he and the *Ocean Belle* had come to the end of their sailing." (Evelyn Richardson, "The Cruise of the Ocean Belle", *Dalhousie Review*, XXIX, No. 1, p.7.)

Lof: Hesitant, reluctant. A mother said of her son's reluctance to return to university, "He's awful lof to go back." Of stormy weather that lingers for days, "It seems lof to clear."

Loft: A room, usually unfinished, on the upper floor of a house, used for storage; in a barn, the upper floor used for the storage of hay, the "hayloft." A "sail loft," a large building where sails are made and repaired.

Lofty: Big feeling. "He's lofty and tonguey."

Log: A slip from a plant or shrub with a leaf bud that will grow.

Logy, loggy: A person who is slow and dull; of a boat, slow-moving, heavy in the waves.

Lollard, loller: A useless, good-for-nothing person, who "lolls" around doing nothing.

Long splice: A name given by the New England settlers to a boat which had been lengthened by cutting it in two, drawing the two sections apart and splicing them together with a "long splice." They would also "long splice" two pieces of rope for one long piece of rope.

Longwithe: A long pole that connects the forward and hind wheels of a cart. Also coupling pole.

Lounder: As used on Cape Island, a severe blow; a hard punch; a heavy clap of thunder.

Lowance: A portion of food placed on a plate as a serving. In Blanche, guests were told, "Everybody helps himself at my table. I don't lowance the food."

Lummock: A useless person. "Why do you put up with that lummock?" an old aunt was asked who was burdened with a lazy niece.

Lump of spruce: A poorly designed and built vessel was referred to as a "lump of spruce." (*Coast Guard*, February 23, 1933.) Another way to refer to a poorly designed and built vessel "A slight departure from the log."

Lunch break: An unpainted streak in the paint left by the painter. Also called a "holiday."

Lunch up: On board a fishing vessel, a "lunch up" was a snack between meals. "In the forecastle all have free access to the 'shack cupboard' where the cook is expected to keep a supply of food for any who wish to 'lunch up' between meals." (*Down Shore Tales*, p. 67.) Today a "lunch up" is a "mug up."

Lur'd day, looard: When the wind is blowing towards the land.

M

Main: To those who live on the islands off the Shelburne County coast, the mainland is the "main." In a letter a person who lived on one of the islands wrote, "We never get a cold until we go to the main." About Seal Island, Archibald MacMechan wrote, "Many a fisherman found there shelter for his boat and lodging for himself. Many a shipwrecked sailor was generously cared for until he could be ferried over to the main."

Mare's egg: A name given in Lower Ohio to "water-rolled weed balls," as they have been described, found on the shores of Lake Deception. The balls are made of debris, tree spills, sand, and twigs, rolled and turned in the sand on the shore by the waves as they are washed back and forth on the shore into the shape of an egg.

Marvel, marvelled: To move or to stroll slowly. "I said to the dog, `You go in the bedroom,' and he marvelled off." "He took a block and I, a rope, and up we marvelled aloft." (*Following the Sea*, p. 29.)

Mash, mish: Marsh, low-lying land edging the shore, much of it covered with saltwater as the tides flow inward; drained by "guzzle holes" as the tide recedes. Marshland was eagerly sought as part of a land grant for its salt marsh hay for oxen.

Mauger, moger: An all-over, miserable, sick feeling. A word that perhaps came from the French word *maigre,* lean, thin.

Measly: Anything of poor quality, as a measly bag of apples.

Meeting: A church service. Tea meeting: a supper to raise money for a church or for some project beneficial to a community.

Middling: A half-well feeling. "How ya feelin'?" "Fair to middling."

Milkmaid's path: The Milky Way.

Mind: To remember. "I mind well the night the Blanche struck the Half Moon."

Miscellaneous: A one-room school where all the children from beginners to grade 11 attended, with one teacher for all grades.

Mitten: To break an engagement. "After all these years of goin' together, she gave him the mitten."

Moger: *See* Mauger.

Monkey doddler: A begetter of illegitimate children.

Mooch, mooching: Loafing around not doing anything of importance.

Moose muffle (muffle stew): A stew made from the fleshy meat around the nostrils of a moose.

Mort: A great many, as a mort of apples; if one works very hard, one accomplishes "a mort of work."

Mosey along: To walk along leisurely.

Muckle: To seize and hold fast to a rope or chain; to latch on to something with a firm grip.

Mud room: the back entry where children are told to "wipe off your feet."

Muddled steak: Stew made from steak.

Mummychug: To cuddle a baby.

Musceline: Muscular strength. In the old days "traps were hauled while under sail, or with small boats, musceline was the motive power used." (*Coast Guard,* April 30, 1936.)

Muster: To put together a meal of odds and ends.

Mustered: To move about without assistance. One old lady who had suffered a stiff knee, boasted that she mustered along with a cane.

N

Nail her to the pin: To hold a vessel on a fixed course, at the highest speed. From the master of a vessel in distress came a plea for assistance, and the response from his rescuer, from the desk of his vessel, that he would "nail her to the pin," full speed ahead. (*Coast Guard,* April 10, 1985.)

Nanny tassels: Sheep manure. Nanny tassel tea was used as an old home remedy to "drive out the measles."

Nary: Not one, as in the old expression, "Three candles burning and nary a ship at sea."

Natter: One who nags others; one who complains endlessly.

Nigh: A word used with a variety of meaning. Close by, "Mother is nigh." Close-fisted, "She's nigh with her pennies." The mental process of remembering, "We proceeded on our way home, arrived in Lockeport July 25th, as nigh as I remember." (*Coast Guard,* March 12. 1931.)

Nip and tuck: The way one must live when times are hard. An old woman remembered when she was a young girl, "It was nip and tuck in those days. Mother worked hard to make both ends meet."

Nippers: A thick band of knitted white wool worn around the palm of the hand by lobstermen when hauling lobster pots.

Noggin: A small cup or a homemade wooden mug. A noggin of hot buttered rum was administered for a chill.

No-see-ums: Very small gnats and flies.

Novies: An American name for the Cape Islanders, the fish boats designed and built on Cape Island.

Nubbin: A green hand at fishing. Also anything small and undeveloped as apples and potatoes.

Nummie: A derogatory term for a person who is deemed slow or of low intelligence.

Nuzzle: A nozzle. *See* Roundy.

O

Off from on; on from off: To those who live on Cape Sable Island, "off" is the mainland; "on" is the island. If you are just "on from off," you have just returned from the mainland; if just "off from on," you are on the mainland from the island. With "on" and "off" are the expressions. "Off again, on again, gone again Gallagher," "On again, gone again, Finnigan."

Oil skins: Waterproof garments made of factory cotton soaked in raw linseed oil with boiled oil added to hasten the process of drying, the linseed oil mixed with yellow ochre or lamp or coal black for colour. *See* Sea Lore.

Ol' hell: An expression of happiness. "When the crew knew they would be rescued 'We were happy as ol' hell.'" (*Coast Guard*, June 20, 1989.)

Ol' pogies: An early variety of the blue potato, that were long and narrow and streaked with purple-blue lines. They grew well in a "lazy bed" of eel grass, rock weed, and kelp, wedged between the stumps of trees as the land was being cleared.

Old: A term of endearment used between husband and wife, "old woman," "old man." A young man spoke of his young wife as "old woman." To which the young wife responded, "I call him 'old man' just like he calls me 'old woman.' I guess he likes me when he calls me 'old woman.'" Sons speak of their fathers as "old man." One remembering the lean years of his childhood, "Never had no boats. The old man couldn't buy them." (*The Lockeport Lockout*, p. 2.) A young fisherman on Cape Island said of his father, "All right, old man, you do it. You sink the traps. You know where to go." (*Voice of the Pioneer* p. 75.) A young man in Coffinscroft told his young wife, "Old woman, if there's a ghost around looking in the windows, we'll follow his footprints in the wet mud." A man remembered when he was a child he called his adopted father and mother, "old man" and "old woman."

Old Davy: Spirit of the deep sea, a variation of Davy Jones, as in Davy Jones' Locker, at the bottom of the sea. "They (the whales) may go and pay old Davy a visit," Captain James Doane Coffin wrote in his whaling journal of the *Margaret Rait,* when the hold of his whaler was nearly filled with the oil he had sailed the long way to the Pacific to obtain. (*Journal of the Margaret Rait*, p. 67.)

Old dear: A term of affection for a friendly older person. "She's an old dear."

Old man's whiskers: *See* Plant Lore.

Old pilgrim: A wise old person with years of living and observing.

Old stick: A grim, straight-laced person.

Old whim: An old belief tinged with superstition.

On the beach: Retired seaman. "On many afternoons old seafarers now on the beach because of age drop in to yarn around the pot-bellied stove." (*Coast Guard,* June 30, 1955.)

On the shelf: Retired, no longer working.

On the shore: The inshore fishing grounds. A young wife was asked where her husband was fishing. She replied, "He's on the shore."

One-lunger: A one-cylinder gasoline engine used in fish boats.

Onnery: Stubborn, pig-headed.

Open banded: The fine single strand of homespun yarn used to knit Sunday stockings.

Outside fisherman: One who fishes offshore, beyond the inshore fishing grounds.

Over the bay: Intoxicated.

Overfalls: In seaman's terms, turbulent water swelling and breaking over submerged rocks and shoals.

Over there: The New England States, the Boston States, where many trekked to find work when there was no work for them in the communities where they lived.

Override the waves: To stem the tide, to go forward against a heavy sea. "The tide running against the wind then blowing had made the sea too rough for his little "skiff to override the waves." (*Down Shore Tales*, p. 50.)

Owl: A freight train in the 1920s with one passenger car attached to rear of the train that "hooted" its way eastward in the early evening, and "hooted" its way west to Yarmouth the next morning, laden with freight and passengers.

Owly: Grumpy, disagreeable.

Own cousin: A first cousin, a son or daughter of an aunt or uncle.

Own son: A son by marriage rather than a stepson, an adopted son, or a son "brought up." "He was one of the old time fishing skippers ... his crew his own sons." (*Down Shore Tales*, p.17.)

Oxtrail, Oxwagon road: A narrow, rough trail cut through the woods for oxen to haul timber from the woodlots. Also known as a "sled road," "wood road," "hauling road," "tote road."

Ox haul: A competition of oxen hauling a heavy drag laden with stones.

P

Pantry: In most of the older houses there was a pantry, a small room set aside for the storage of food and with shelves for dishes. At a pantry sale were sold home-baked cakes and bread, pickles and jams.

Parlour: The living-room, the front room. In many of the homes the parlour was used only for special occasions, for weddings and funerals and when the minister called, and was tightly closed, the window blinds drawn to keep the sunlight from fading the roses in the rug. In a lobster pot, the parlour is a compartment where the lobster crawls through a "roundy" or "nuzzle bow," and cannot escape.

Patch fox: A red fox with patches of brown and grey. A cross fox, a red fox with a black stripe down its back and across its shoulders.

Patter: Empty chatter.

Pea bouncer: A wide-brimmed lady's hat.

Pea pod: A very small one-man boat. On Forbes Point when the church was burned, it was decided everyone should earn a dollar to rebuild their church. Each was to tell how the dollar was earned. One young man wrote a verse to go with his dollar.

> *I went out fishing in my little pea pod,*
> *and earned my dollar for the house of God.*

Pea souper: A very heavy fog.

Pea stick: A nickname for a tall, slender woman.

Peaked (Pea kid): Thin and sickly, especially a thin, sickly child.

Pension: An old crippled bird. *See* Bird Lore.

Pent road: A private road closed with a gate or with bars to keep cattle from straying on the public highway.

Pepper buds: The pods of red pepper. As punishment for "swear words" a boy in Clarks Harbour had to "stand on the platform and chew `pepper buds.'" (*Down Shore Tales*, p. 25.)

Perished: To die of the cold. In Lockeport following the wreck of a small fish boat and the loss of one of her crew came word, "He did not drown, he perished."

Perishing: Extremely cold weather. "After several days of perishing cold and heart-breaking labour they worked the *Ocean Belle* in to Bay St. George." (Evelyn Richardson, "The Cruise of the Ocean Belle," *Dalhousie Review Vol IXIX*, No. 1 p.7.)

Persuader: A ruler or pointer used by a teacher "to persuade youngsters to mind."

Pickings: Goods salvaged from a wreck. A little girl remembered her father came from a "wrack, and in his little boat filled with pickings there was a silver sugar spoon."

Pig eye: A shooting star.

Pig potatoes: Small potatoes put aside as food for pigs.

Pigs to market: Snoring, as in driving his pigs to market. As one little boy defined snoring, "sleeping out loud."

Piggin: A wooden mug made of staves, one stave higher than the rim for a handle. It was used to dip water from a bucket and to bail a boat.

Piles: *See* Spikes.

Pingeons: Painful sores. *See* Sea Lore.

Pink wink: A spring peeper.

Pinkie, pink: A small sailboat, sharp both ends, which was used for fishing and in the coasting trade.

Pint: A point of land. One described "pint" as a neck of land. In Sandy Point, one hears "a pint of land, a point of rum."

Pissabed: Dandelion

Pitch pole: The ungainly gait of a bear going downhill.

Pitching in: Helping. When men fished from little boats they often needed help from others, as one related when his boat was partly burned, "If it hadn't been for my friends pitching in, I might have lost the whole season." (*Voice of the Pioneer*, p. 73.)

Plagued mean: Stingy. "He's too plagued mean to live."

Platform: When salt hay was used as winter fodder for oxen, a platform of rails was mounted on posts driven into the marsh to hold the platform well above high tide. The rails were placed well apart to allow the air to circulate through the hay to prevent mildew. A tall pole stood in the centre of the platform around which the hay was stacked in a high rounded pyramid. Sometimes a piece of canvas was tied down over the hay.

Plumb: An intensifier, expressing extremes. "I'm plumb worn out." "He's plumb crazy."

Pobbles: Rounded beach stones made smooth with the rolling tides.

Pod: Used in Sandy Point by an old sea captain for a slow moving person too lifeless to move "out of his own shadow."

Pogie: Unemployment Insurance benefits.

Poison neat: A house kept so neat and tidy, it irritates others.

Political muggerwumpery: Political partisanship and patronage as practised by various political parties. (Editorial, *Coast Guard*, May 5, 1955.)

Pole load: A small haystack that can be lifted on two poles slid beneath the stack and carried into the barn for storage in the hay mow.

Pollywog: A tadpole.

Poor man's fertilizer: The first light fall of snow after the return of the robins in the spring. It will soon melt and carry nutrients down into the earth and fertilize the soil for planting. It is also known as the "robin's snow," for as it melts into the earth, the worms move upward into the waiting beaks of the robins.

Pooty: A person slow in speech and action. "A man down Ingomar way was always called Old Pooty. If you went down the road and Old Pooty was working in his potato piece and you called, 'How you doin' Pooty,' it would be next day before Old Pooty would be just about ready to answer."

Popple: The silver poplar; the white poplar.

Port La Bear: An anglicized interpretation of the old French placename Port à l'ours or Port aux ours, evidently so named for bears seen along the wooded shores of the harbour. One school girl thought the name was Portly Bear.

Portland breeze: A heavy wind storm, one with the force of the gale that wrecked the *City of Portland* in Boston Bay.

Pot smasher: A very severe storm at sea that smashes lobster pots and rolls them ashore in the heavy tides.

Pounded: To force a boat forward. Those going to rescue a fisherman in distress, "pounded their boat to get there." (*Coast Guard*, October 17, 1989.)

Pounding: Driving hard and fast. "Come the deer season there will be some pounding up and down the road."

Power: A great many. A fisherman reported that he "lost a power of traps in a storm." A great amount. "He must have a power of money."

Pram: A small, flat-bottomed boat, smaller than a punt, but square at each end, used for duck hunting. Also known as a "box boat."

Prayer handles: Knees. "He bent down on his prayer handles and thanked the Lord for fish and potatoes."

Prayer windows: *See* Eyebrow windows.

Preacher: Local name for the Great Black-backed Gull.

Precious little: A small amount. "She had precious little in her purse."

Prong fork: A long-handled, two or three-tine fork used as a hay or barn fork, or as a fish fork to pitch fish from a boat into boxes.

Puckerstring: A drawstring on a bag.

Putter: To spend one's time doing things of no consequence.

Q

Quassia cup: A cup or goblet turned from quassia wood used for medicinal purposes. *See* Home Remedies.

Quid: Portion of tobacco cut from the plug for chewing; also, a cud of tobacco.

Quills: The sharp, needle-like leaves of the pine trees.

Quite: Used as an intensifier, as in "quite many were there."

R

Rabbit: A piece of furniture, a table, a stool, made from odd pieces of wood or boards "scrounged" from a pile of refuse lumber or discarded boards.

Rack, racked: To search for an answer. "I racked my brain trying to think what to say next."

Raft: Many. A raft of ducks. A raft of old stories. A raft of ice: great cakes of ice piled one upon another.

Rags: Old and worn clothing. "We were happy as long as there was enough to eat, and a few rags to wear, and a boat so we could get out and catch the fish. What more does a man want?" (*Voice of the Pioneer*, p.75.)

Rare: Rear, as a horse rears.

Redd: To clean and tidy up a house.

Reise: To rise up. An elderly lady who lived alone heard a strange sound in the night. She told her granddaughter, "When I heard the strange sound I reise up in bed to see what was in the dark."

Right: Used as an intensifier for "very." "She's right pretty, right perky, right smart, lively and in good health and of good spirit."

Rimed: To fuss and fume. "My dog, he rimed and rimed all night."

Rimrack: To search thoroughly; to turn things upside down.

Rinctum: A rage; a temper tantrum. A nurse who cared for an old woman told her friends, "When she gets in one of her rinctums, I just get up and walk off." In Green Harbour, a "rinctum diddy" is a specially violent fit of temper. A mother told her friend, "My boy he's in a rinctum diddy."

Ring the woods: To spread out through the woods and encircle the deer so they cannot escape.

Ripper: A violent winter storm with heavy wind and snow.

Road, on the: The baby in the womb. A man of short stature was heard to say, "I don't know why they didn't add three or four inches to me while I was on the road."

Rob roy: A lean-to porch built to protect the outside door of a house.

Rode: A rope attached to the bow of a boat to secure it to an anchor or mooring post.

Rooching: *See* Rutching.

Rooster: A swirling ventilator on a chimney pipe.

Rote, rute: The sound of the bow waves as they sweep against the shore; the sound of waves breaking on the shore.

Round fish: Fresh cod or haddock, headed and gutted but not split open as for salting or drying.

Roundy: A hoop made of a pliable spruce twig or of witherod, knit into the meshes of the pothead through which a lobster crawls. Also known as a "nuzzle bow." *See* Sea Lore.

Rouse: A vigorous pull. A woman from Woods Harbour was overheard to say, "I fetched the cretur a rouse and her tail came off."

Rowen: A second crop of hay cut in late August or early September.

Rubbed: To survive hard times. "With a few dollars ... I have rubb'd through the winter." (Sarah Lewis, *Annals,* p. 69.)

Rule: Recipe for cooking.

Run: In placenames, a swift running brook: Bakers Run, Stalkers Run.

Rustle: To prepare something in a hurry. "I can soon rustle a meal together."

Rusty pork: Rancid pork.

Rutching: To make a great noise when moving around. Also rooching.

S

Sad cake: Soggy, heavy cake.

Sail dragger: A captain who carries too much sail for the safety of his vessel.

Sailorizing: Sailing. "Many men living along our shores have been on the water either sailorizing or fishing." (*Coast Guard*, November 3, 1939.)

Sailors' Graveyard: When many ships were lost along the shores of Hemeon's Head and on nearby reefs, many bodies washed ashore and were buried in Little Harbour giving to the tiny community the name Sailors' Graveyard.

Salt horse: Beef cured in brine. "In the old days, 'salt horse' and 'hard tack' were the chief items in the sailors' diet." (*Down Shore Tales*, p. 70.)

Salt lick: Hard marsh mud covered with a layer of salt left by the receding tide where wild animals come from the woods for a lick of salt.

Saltmarsh milk: Milk from a cow that had grazed on a salt marsh. "Soon as you started to milk and smell it—you knew you had a bucket of milk you couldn't sell."

Salvors: Those who salvaged cargoes from wrecks.

Sam Hill: To go very fast as in the expression "to go like Sam Hill." "Saw three whales going to windward like Sam Hill." (PANS, Journal of the *Athol*, Manuscript.) In more recent years the term is sometimes "sand hill." "What in sand hill is going on around here?"

Sand snake: A hollow tube sewn from cloth filled with sand placed along the bottom of an outside door to prevent drafts.

Sandy spits: Areas of sand that rise above the level of the ebb tide. "One can walk quite a distance on the sandy spits when the tide is out."

Savanna, savannah: An open expanse of level land, moist but not wet or soggy as a swamp, covered with a scattering of stunted black spruce and hackmatack, and a ground cover of kilkid, swamp laurel, Indian pitcher plants and bog cotton.

Save the tide: To take advantage of the flow of the tide, outward bound on the ebb; inward bound on the flood.

Scabs: Lichens that grow on rocks.

Scat: Scared. "I wasn't born in the woods to be scat by an owl."

Scoff: 1. To make disappear. A heavy windstorm that will scoff (blow) the clouds away. 2. To eat quickly. "He soon scoffed it down."

Scooch: To crouch; to stoop. To "scooch down" to spy and to be caught "scooching" is an unpardonable misdemeanour.

Scrabble net: A rope ladder with the wooden bars knotted to the rope, used to rescue survivors to the deck of a vessel.

Scrod: Anything of poor quality and of little value as a low trump card in the game of 45s.

Scringe: Cringe. "The noise made me scringe."

Scrounge, scrounger, scrounged: To search leftovers and make do with what can be found.

Scrunch, scrunchy: The crunching sound of snow or ice crushed under foot.

Scud: Describes fog coming in from the sea over the land. "A scud of fog hid the house."

Scudding: Sculling.

Scuffs: Old shoes worn about the barn, or when gardening, or in a fish boat.

Scun: To shirk one's duties, as in "to scun-off"; to trim another in a game of contest, "He scun me a mile."

Sea turn: A fine clear day. "The day had been fine and clear, with only a moderate wind and sea, a day called by the fishermen, 'A sea turn.'" (*Down Shore Tales*, p. 3.)

Set: Sit. "Come in and set down."

Set to: A fight.

Setting: A nest full of eggs to be hatched by a "settin' hen."

Shabang: Everybody. "The whole shabang was there."

Shack, shacking: Fishing term for cod, hake, and herring. When fishing for shack, a fisherman is shacking.

Shack cupboard: On the old fishing vessels the cupboard where the cook kept a supply of food for the crew. *See* Lunch up.

Shack it off: To shake bait from a fish hook. A fisherman of Cape Island explained the term. "When the fish hooks on a tub of trawl are baited and something happens that the bait is not used, the fishermen shack it off to rebait."

Shadow decoys, silhouette decoys: Decoys floated from the bow or stern of a boat to attract ducks flying above them. On Cape Island such decoys are called shadow decoys; in Coffinscroft, silhouette decoys.

Shallop harbour: A deep-water inlet where the small boats of the early settlers could be anchored for shelter from heavy tides and wind storms.

Shaped shingle, fancy shingles: Shingles cut at the lower edge to form a pattern when nailed to a house for "fancy work." They are cut in a number of different patterns: a semi-circle for feathered shingles or fish scales; a single sharp point for diamond; others are cut with a scalloped edge or with fine sharp points.

Sharp shooter: A fishing vessel with a sharp bow built for speed, such as the clipper schooners designed to bring fish directly to market, fresh. A sharp shooter is also know as a "file bottom."

Shaving mill: An old name for an American privateer, some not more than an open boat, that preyed upon fishermen and other vessels at sea along the South Shore of Nova Scotia, and robbed their fish houses and their homes. As to why the term was used, an old man in Barrington replied, with a chuckle, "Because the crew was a gang of bearded ruffians who needed to be rolled through a shaving mill to scrape off their beards."

She-shall-burn: Before Port Roseway was renamed Shelburne by Governor Parr, there is an old story that one of the rowdy settlers in the new town was pushed into a boat and rowed out to sea. As he was rowed down the long reach of the harbour he stood in the stern of the boat with clenched fists, shouting, "She-shall-burn. She-shall-burn."

Shellacking: A tongue lashing. "Did she ever give me a shellacking."

Shimmy: A woman's vest or undershirt.

Shindig, shinding: A noisy affair, a rumpus.

Shiver: A sever bump or blow on the head.

Ship's husband: One who was engaged to sail on foreign voyages as agent for the ship's owner.

Shooting a breeze: Everybody in a room talking at the same time.

Shore captain: Captain of a tug boat that trudges along close to the shore.

Shoreman: The partner in a fishing business who looks after the business ashore.

Shy: Exiguous, missing. A father in Sandy Point said to his spendthrift daughter whose purse was always empty, "I suppose you're shy again." A woman culling her silverware remarked, "I'm shy on forks."

Shy, shied: A mild courtship. "He used to shy around Annie. Before Annie, he shied around her sister."

Sick bread: Toast. When bread had to be toasted before an open fire or on top of a wood-burning stove, it was seldom made except for the sick, as a 'binder' for diarrhoea, or when burnt black, to sweeten an upset stomach.

Sile: Seal.

Singsong: A gathering of friends to sing hymns and old songs.

Sink room: In older homes the small room off the kitchen and near the back door with a "dry sink" made of wood, with a hole to pour water through to a pail below the sink.

Sinking: Dying.

Sit: Visit. "I've come to sit." "Come and sit awhile."

Skate of trawl: A tub of trawl line with baited hooks.

Skimpy: Meagre, small, as a skimpy dress, too small to fit well.

Skinny-be-links: A very skinny, thin person.

Skipper: Master of a fishing boat or a small trading vessel.

Skun: To bruise or skin a knee or leg.

Slack water, ebb-tide slack: Between tides, when the water is relatively motionless, "We were able to find our way around in the thickest fog and to keep on one or other of the best fishing spots for an hour or two at 'slack water' which is the best time for handline fishing." (*Down Shore Tales*, p. 43.)

Slap jacks: Rubber boots cut off and worn as low shoes.

Slash: Slush.

Slat: To hurl or throw with force.

Slat bed: A wooden bed. The supporting framework is fitted with wooden slats across the frame to support a mattress or a bed tick filled with straw or feathers. Sometimes the slats were removed and holes drilled in the frame and lashed with rope when the bed became a "cord bed."

Sleepers: The sandy deposit in the corner of the eyelids after sleeping.

Slew: A great number, a great amount; a slew of people.

Slinky: Thin, lean; a "slinky" cat.

Sliver, to: To slice or fillet as meat, fish, cake, etc.

Slooping: Moving. He was "slooping around in the cracked ice and fish curry (gurry) that was on the floor, in his bare feet." (*The Lockeport Lookout,* p. 2.)

Slosh: To be thrown around by the waves. "The boat would need hefty repairs after a slosh in salt water." (*Coast Guard,* May 15, 1985.)

Slue: An old seaman's term to twist or turn, to shift, as in the wind.

Slugg ice: Partly melted, broken ice floating on the surface of the water.

Sluiced off: To slide accidentally into water. "He was slopping along the shore and sluiced off into the water."

Smackers: Dollars. "No doubt the tow would have cost a few hundred smackers." (*Coast Guard,* May 15, 1985.)

Smart: Active and in good health. "He's right smart for an old fella."

Smidgen: A sliver, a very small amount, as in a "smidgen" of pie, a "smidgen" of cloth.

Smile: A flat smooth rock used in a stone wall to level the layers of rock.

Smoke house: A tall, slender structure of wood where fish are smoked over a smudge fire of chips and sawdust, with tussocks of ferns sometimes added for a special flavour.

Smokin' oakum: An expression of surprise.

Smooched: Smeared. "He was smooched with mud where he fell in the bog."

Smother: To fly in close together. "The birds come up and smother right in." ("Shooting Ducks at the Half Moons," *Island Echoes*, p.91.)

Smuggling pumpkins: A young girl pregnant with an illegitimate child is said to be smuggling pumpkins.

Snags: Old boots worn by woodsmen when working among the "snags" of old roots and stumps of trees when clearing a woodlot.

Snags: Broken teeth.

Sneakers, Cape Island: Hip rubber boots worn by fishermen.

Snick: A very small piece, a sliver, as in a snick of cake.

Sniffing bowl: A bowl or goblet filled with hot brandy and sniffed for the fumes from the brandy for relief from a stuffy nose.

Snippy: 1. Cold and frosty, of weather. 2. Critical and superior, of people.

Snuff: Not in good form. "Not up to snuff," refers to ill health. "She doesn't keep the house up to snuff," refers to housekeeping.

Sny: Mean, especially with money.

Sod bridge: A low causeway constructed over a bog or damp land of rocks covered with sods.

Some: Very. "Some smart."

Soppings: Bread or dumplings used to "sop" up the gravy in a duck stew. One old lady on Cape Island declared that she didn't like the duck, but she dearly loved the soppings.

Spanking new: Brand new. Something dashing and pretty and new, not worn or used before, such as a "spanking new" dress.

Spatlatches: White spats that came up to the knees.

Spell: A period of time. "The men would come over from their boats and help me for a spell."

Spile: 1. A log or piece of squared timber built into the side of a wharf that extends above the wharf as a mooring post for boats. 2. Heavy posts or logs driven into mud and sand to mark a safe channel of water over sand and mudflats 3. Posts to hold a fish weir.

Spills: The sharp, needle-like leaves of the conifers.

Spin-off: A person who spins yarns, old tales.

Spin top: A specially designed lobster pot buoy that spins with the currents or waves.

Spleeny: 1. Inclined to be grouchy and ill-tempered. 2. To make more of an ailment than is warranted. Even "a dog can be spleeny if you spoil him."

Split-the-wind: A long, sharp gable roof. As a nickname, a person with a long, thin, sharp nose, Jimmy Split-the-wind.

Spngle, sprngle: To spread out in all directions.

Spring lake: A lake fed by springs, in contrast to a "sunk lake," one in a swamp.

Spring lines: Ropes attached to the bow or to the quarter of a boat which hold the boat in a stable position. "The two boats were sprung apart with spring lines, and were very stable." (*Coast Guard*, July 9, 1985.)

Spondulance: Money.

Spotters: Those who watch from the mast for swordfish.

Spouter: A whaling vessel. "They (two vessels) are both working to windward, probably spouters in the same tedious predicament as ourselves." (*Journal of the Margaret Rait*, p. 23.)

Spruce, lump of: An old term of contempt for a poorly designed and constructed vessel.

Spruced up: Smartly dressed or refurbished.

Spue: To eject; to force outward.

Spudge: A three-tine fish spear.

Square away, squared away: To put everything in order, everything "ship-shape," in response to the shipboard command to "square away and let her go."

Squareboard: Shipbuilder's term for a carvel-built vessel, the planks of her hull flush with her seams, the boards placed "square" upon each other for a smooth hull.

Squire: From esquire, used as a title of respect for a justice of the peace, merchants, teachers, the title applied to the Christian name, as Squire Jim.

Squirmers: Eels.

Stalls: A thick covering for the palm of the hand worn by fishermen to prevent chafing when hauling fish nets and lobster pots.

Stark calm: The sea and the wind are motionless.

Staving: An old name for wainscot when made of boards cut like barrel staves. *See* Deep base board.

Stay the stomach: To sustain one's strength with food, from an old meaning for "stay"—to sustain with strength; to support from sinking.

Steaming: To move forward very quickly, as a boat steaming full speed ahead. "She was observed shortly before 2 p.m. steaming into the harbour with a brig in tow." (*Coast Guard*, February 23, 1933.)

Stem the tide: To overcome the strength of the tide when sailing or rowing a boat. A fisherman of Cape Island remembered when he was fishing in a little boat and the tide turned, "It was all I could do to stem the tide."

Stepped out: To die suddenly. "Old so and so sure stepped out quick."

Sternfull: A good catch of fish. "The lad that day had been out alone in a dory, and had secured a good sternfull of fish." (*Coast Guard*, November 3, 1939.)

Sticker: The man who throws the harpoon at a whale or swordfish.

Sticking tommy, sticking tom: A metal, funnel-shaped candle holder which was used on fish boats to provide light.

Stiffled: Tough steak or meat cooked in a pan with gravy.

Stinted islands: In early township records some islands were set aside as commons, as pasture land for sheep and pigs, the number of animals on each island regulated by an overseer appointed by the proprietors of the township.

Stived: Confined in close quarters.

Stiver: To stagger, to sway as when carrying a heavy load, "All I could stiver under." In Trench's study, of *English Past and Present*, "stiver" is listed as an old Dutch sea term that found its way into the English language.

Stoop: A platform or steps leading to an entrance door, usually covered with a porch roof.

Stopple: A cork or glass stopper for a bottle.

Stormstayed: Prevented from continuing a journey because of bad weather, as summer birds caught in a storm during migration and forced to remain for weeks or months in their summer homeland.

Stove, stove in, stoven: To break, damage, crush with force. "The keeper's boat was stove in, the cellar of the house filled with salt water." (*Coast Guard*, March 1931.)

Straight out: To work exceedingly hard. "I've been working straight out for a week—no lazin' around at the plant."

Stranger: A unborn baby. "She's expecting a little stranger."

Strapbasket: Lunch or food baskets with straps to go over the shoulders.

Straw boss: One who looks on as others work.

Stringpiece: An old term for the heavy squared timber around the edge of a dock or wharf. "I made a jump in the dark, off the string piece of the wharf, and fortunately landed in the rigging, got down on deck, tiptoed to my bunk and turned in." (*Following the Sea*, p. 31.) *Also* Caplog.

Strip bed: A wooden bed with narrow strips of canvas nailed across the frame to support the feather or hay-filled bed tick.

Strippings: The last milk drawn from a cow's udder when milking.

Stroke oar: The oar that sets the pace for rowing.

Stuff: Some refer to home-grown vegetables as "stuff." One in Shelburne who grew vegetables in his garden, said, "The old folks they used to keep their stuff in a root cellar. I've got my stuff upstairs in the house."

Stuffing: Energy. "He knocked the stuffing out of me."

Suit of sails: The sails for ship. An old Shelburne sailmaker when asked how long it had been since he made a "set of sails," replied, "My friend, it is not a 'set of sails,' it is a 'suit of sails.'" (*Coast Guard*, June 30, 1955.)

Sunday throat: "Did something go down your Sunday throat?" A query when someone is choking on a crumb.

Sundown flocks: The flocks of seabirds that fly down the long reach of a harbour at sundown to their nighttime roosts.

Sunk lake: A lake in a swamp.

Sunken ledges: Shoals well below tide level over which the sea washes without breaking.

Suntag: An old name in Barrington for a triangular shawl worn by old ladies.

Sut: Soot.

Swallow the anchor: To retire from going to sea.

Swonked: Mentally and physically exhausted from hard labour, a local adaptation of "swamped."

T

Tad: A little boy. "A grand little tad."

Tags: Alder catkins.

T'aint: Contraction for "it is not."

Takel: Tackle in block and tackle. Sometimes a block and tackle are referred to as "blocks." When something is to be lifted, "Bring the blocks."

Tan toasting: A tanning; a spanking.

Tatter toddle: Meat chowder with "tatters"(potatoes).

Tea chest: A large, square rock on the eastern shores of Shelburne Harbour at Lower Sandy Point that resembles a wooden chest in which loose tea was imported from China.

Tea kettle: Steamer. A seaman's term of contempt for the first steamers that came puffing along the shores.

Tea meeting: A church or community supper with an abundance of food.

Tell tail: A gossip, a tattletail, from the nautical "tell tail," an instrument on a vessel to "tell" the position of the tiller.

Tempest: A thunderstorm.

Tending 'round: Frequently seen in a certain locality, an animal, a bird, a person. A young man courting a young lady.

Thank-you-mam: A bump in a road that makes one's head bob up and down, as if saying, "Thank-you-mam."

Thatch: A good crop of hair.

Thimble: The flue iron in a chimney.

Thinking tacks: Capacity to think. In the *Coast Guard*, March 12, 1931, a correspondent ran out of ideas and ended his letter, "But I desist, for our thinking tacks are not aboard."

Thole pins: Wooden pegs set in the gunwale of a boat to hold the oars in place. *See* Tinkers.

Thrum: In place names, a point of land partially covered with water at high tide; also small islands near the shore, as in One Tree Thrum near Sherose Island.

Thunder struck: Struck dumb with astonishment.

Tick: A mattress for a slat or cord bed made from ticking, a closely woven feather-proof cloth, filled with feathers, for a feather-tick, the warmest and cosiest of all the bed ticks; with hay, and sometimes eelgrass.

Ticket: An unkempt person dressed in disreputable clothes. "She's a hard lookin' old ticket."

Tickle: The V bottom on a small boat.

Ticklish: Not dependable; unreliable, as a business deal may be a ticklish venture.

Tidahvate: To dress up to make oneself look smart and attractive.

Tiddly: Unstable; a tiddly person; a tiddly boat.

Tin ear: Unable to distinguish different musical notes. "He has a tin ear. He can't tell one note from another, and he sings in the choir."

Tingling: To swish the back of the legs with an alder switch as a mild form of punishment.

Tingling rage: A temper tantrum.

Tinkers: Small, undersized lobsters; small mackerel, also known as thole pins.

Tire: A sleeveless coverall made of cotton print or linen, buttoned at the back and worn by girls to keep their dresses spotless.

Tits up: To have fallen upon one's back when drunk is to lie "tits up."

Titters: A fine rash of water blisters.

Tizick: An old name for consumption, and for a chest cold or asthma. *Also* tissicky, as in "tissicky cough."

Toad stabber: A jack knife.

Toed-off: When knitting socks the toe of the sock is toed-off.

Togged up: Dressed up with fancy clothes.

Toller: A special breed of dogs that have been trained to attract ducks and other sea birds within range of the hunter's gun.

Tom Doty: To be a "Tom Doty" is to eat a lot. *See also* Ben Dodie.

Tombstone: The transom of a dory which in shape resembles a tombstone.

Toothpick schooner: A schooner of slender sheer, built for speed.

Top dressing: Manure spread over a hay field as fertilizer.

Tother: The other. "He doesn't know tother from which."

Tracadie: A blood relative, rather than a relative by marriage, especially one with a strong family resemblance to others of the same family.

Train: Fuss and fume. "My dog trained all night."

Traipse: To roam around aimlessly.

Trooper: A person who objects strenuously. "She sat up shouting like a trooper."

Trotters: Sheep manure.

Try cakes: Small cakes baked in tiny pans to test a recipe.

Tuck out: A good meal.

Tuckered out: Exhausted.

Tunder: Thunder.

Tunk: To tap sharply as on the side of a metal pail to attract farm animals and hens.

Twilight glass: white milkglass.

Twit: A little boy.

T: To a number of words t is added: "acrost" for across; "She lives acrost the harba"; "gaft" for gaff; "wharft" for wharf; "hand holt" for hand hold, a hold fast. "He was aloft at the masthead doing some work, when he missed a "handholt" and fell a distance of eighty feet." (*Coast Guard*, June 16, 1955.)

U

Uncle: Title of respect for an older man in the community, used with Christian name, as, Uncle Levi, or full name, as Uncle Levi Crowell.

Uncle Wiggley: A twitching reflected light on a wall from a mirror. In Barrington the same reflected light is known as Humpty Dumpty.

Underway: Pregnant. "She was only sixteen when she was underway with Peter."

Under the weather: Not feeling well; half sick.

Upalong: up the shore.

Up the ladder: Getting on in years. "He's quite far up the ladder. Smart for his years."

Uppity: High handed and big feeling.

V

Vinegar twins: Pals.

W

Warming closet: A thin metal closet part of a cook stove through which the stove pipe passed to provide heat to the closet to keep plates and food warm.

Weather glass: A barometer.

Weedy: Not feeling well.

Wee waw: To walk in an uneven gait.

Went away: Died.

Wet your whistle: Have a drink.

Whack: Many; a large amount. A whack of berries; a whack of money.

Whacked: Divided, as money earned by two fishermen fishing together in the same boat. "Whatever we made we still whacked up." (*Coast Guard*, April 4, 1989.)

Wharf rat: A derelict who hangs around a wharf.

What: Used at the end of a sentence for emphasis. "She's some smart, what."

White rose tea: Milk and hot water.

Whitewashed Yankee: A person born in one of the New England States of Canadian parentage; a Nova Scotian who went to the "Boston States" to work and later returned to live in their homeland.

Whitewater lake: A lake fed by springs.

Wicked lot: An over abundance. "Over in the woods there's a wicked lot of mayflowers."

Widow maker: A bowsprit of a sailing vessel from which many a sailor fell when carrying the foot of a sail forward.

Widow's watch: *See* Captain's watch.

Wild scrub: Scrubby trees. "The land was low and wet, and beyond that wild scrub." (*Coast Guard*, February 23, 1933.)

Wind splitter: A house with a sharp gable roof. *See* Split-the-wind.

Winding blades: An old name for a swift used to wind yarn into skeins.

Wingin: Fussing. "Stop your wingin'," an old word remembered as used in Welshtown by a descendant of one of the early Welsh settlers.

Witch's egg: A very small egg without a yolk laid by a hen before her fall moult.

Wood colt: An illegitimate child.

Woold: To wind yarn into a ball, an adaptation of the nautical "woold," to bind rope round a mast or to bind two or more pieces of wood together.

Y

Yaffle: Chew. "Haf' to cover my dahlias with a fish net so the cows won't yaffle 'em off."

Yarn fly: A large fly or bee that comes into houses and schoolrooms in the fall of the year and "bumbles" up and down the window panes with a sound like a spinning wheel. In Barrington the same flies are called fall flies.

Yunder: Yonder; off in the distance. "Over yunder is tomorrow."

INDEX

Acadians 27
Adams, Mary 198
admonition and advice 48
Africa xv
Alder whistle 144
Allendale 11, 19, 66, 75, 104, 181, 194
American Revolution xiv
Americans xiv
amphibians 113
anger knot 60
animal lore 101-107
Ann Street 196
apparitions 15-17
Apple Island 23
April Fool's Day 163
Arbor Day 163-164
Atkinson, Robert 196
August twisters 91
Australia 11, 181

babies 34
Baccaro 77, 84, 104, 183
backen 60, 65-66, 90
bakeapples 115

Ballarat 181
Barrington xii, 70, 80, 111, 115, 132, 140, 143, 156, 171, 181, 183, 187, 192, 195, 197
Barrington Harbour 181
Barrington Passage 4, 17, 18, 21, 69, 134
Barton and Broat, Parish of 196
Battery Hill 27
Bay of Fundy 190
bear biscuit 120
bed ticks 150
Beesling 102, 152
Bell, Almira 188
Benham 195
Benham's Road 195
Bermuda 187
Betsy, Heavens to 52
Big Island 25
Birchtown bay xv
Birchtown xv, 26
bird lore 94-100: crows 95-96; names associated with

INDEX

sounds 97; names of birds 96; sea and shore birds 97-100
birth 33
birthday 34
birthmark 33
Blades, Henry 198
Blanche 104, 188, 189
Blanche Island 188
blockings and stores 173
Blue Island 26
blueberry buckle 152
blueberry fungy 152
boat and shipbuilding 178-180
Bon auger days 45, 159
Bon Portage 100, 152
Boston 172, 193, 194
Boston Harbour 198
boxes 140
Brass Hill 4, 148
bread 42
break a leg 39
breeding sore 59
Brick Hill 26
brooms 31
Brown's barn 47
Brown, David Jeremiah 195
Brown, Capt. Philip 183
buca 59, 73, 114
buckle to 53
burial 157-159
buried treasure 23-28
buttermilk 67, 71

camomile 79

camphor 65, 69, 71, 72, 77, 79
Cap Nègre 166
Cap Nègre, de Sable 166
Cape Breton 172
Cape Canso 171
Cape Island 12, 62, 67, 72, 80, 91, 111, 163, 176, 191, 197
Cape Islander (boat) 178
Cape Negro 167, 193
Cape Negro Harbour 25
Cape Negro Island 25, 191
Cape Sable 27, 84, 167, 190, 191
Cape Sable Island 159, 201
Capstick 194
Caribbean 14
Carleton Village 24, 85
cats 86, 89, 105-106: black cats 42, 105; cat's tooth 38
cattle 36, 39
celebration of days 159-165
changeable silk 192
Charlotte the Witch 20-21
chestnut pipe 145
children's lore 121-145: crafts 144-145; games 140-144; rhymes, verses, and tongue twisters 130-136; skipping rhymes 127-130; stories 136-140
chimney witch 20
Christian doors 39
Christmas 12, 159-161

chum, chumming 172
church mouse 52
Churchover 3, 182
Clam Point mud flat 168
Clarks Harbour 62, 89, 135, 147, 156, 157, 170, 184
clockwise 199
clover 62, 63, 80
cobwebs 68
Cockerwit 99
Coffinscroft 6, 9, 16, 110, 115, 127, 180
coins 26
colours, green 33
compass house 173
cookies and cakes 199
cordials 153
Cork Harbour 196
counting out rhymes 121-127
courtship 156-157
cows and calves 94, 101-102, 106-107
cracklin 153
Cranes Point 151
crows 95-96, 199
Cuba 182
Cuckoo, Black-billed 36, 94
Cunningham, Capt. James 182
cycle of life, birth, childhood, marriage, death 33-37

dandelions 73, 115, 153
days, good and bad luck 32
days of week: Monday 32; Friday 32, 35, 40, 86; Sunday 36, 40, 86
death, omens of 36
death, on the ebb tide 158
decess 180
Dennis (Couchou) 201
Dennis, Capt. James 187
deserters xv, 194-198
devil's gold 27
devil, to frighten the 38
dinner-bah 154
ditty-bag, ditty-box 173-174
Dixon, Jacob 191
Doane, Capt. Warren 181
Doane, Maria 191
Doane, Nathan 191
dogs 86, 105, 106, 189
dont's 39-40
door 31
Dorchester, England 196
dories, bank clipper, double, powder 179
dory fishing 170
dory plugs 152
dory scudding 179
drails 168, 173
dreams 17-18
dunky flunk 152
Dunn's Light 9-10
Dunn's Rock 10
Dutchman, pantaloons 86

INDEX

dyes, homemade 147-148

East Jordan 3, 12
Easter 162-163
ebb tide, ebb tide slack 167-168
Etherington, John 196

fall dandelion 74, 106
Ferguson, William 187
fiddleheads 120
finger and toe nails 37-38, 40
finger rhymes 134-136
fish: 111-113; herring 168; mackerel 168; pollack 168; squid 168
fishing 166-176
flag, to fall 42
flunkies 170
Flying Rock 189
Flynn, Margaret 190
fog loom 89
fog mull 88
fog-eater 88
foods 151-153
fool's hill 49
forerunners 12-15
forks 31
forty-fives, game of 154
Freed Blacks xv
French xiii, 27
Friday, good and bad luck 32
Frude 195

funerals 157-159
fungy 152

games, indoors and outdoors 140-144, 154-155
Gander 13
gannets 168, 202
garden parties 156
ghostly lights 9
ghosts 2-10
ginger plum 72, 114, 153
Glance, Mary 195
glen, glin 84-85
goat's hair 89
God willing 44
gold thread 63, 75, 78, 80
Golden Arm 9, 139-140
Goodwick, Philip 197
Goose Shoot 161
gout 71
Grand Lake 10
Granny 64
grapnel, graplin 175
Gray Island 4, 23, 24
Green Harbour 14, 26, 68, 115, 143, 192
Green Island 26, 179
Green Rock Bar 186
Ground Hog Day 88
ground swell 85
guests, when to expect 31-32
Gull Rock 84
Gull, Black-backed 99
gull, the lone 86, 96, 202

gulls 96, 168
Gunning Cove 3, 196
gurry, and gurry soap 146-147, 172
Guy Fawke's Day 165

hags, haglets 99, 168
Half Moon 189, 191, 193
half clear day 193
Halifax 19, 183, 187
Hallowe'en 164-165
handbarrow 172
Hannah, Shin bone of 52
hard tack 171
Hardy, Joseph 194-195
Hawk, the 123, 124, 133, 143, 147, 167
hens and roosters 104, 107
Hessie, Good day 52
Hibbard's Brook 143, 144
Hitchens, Capt. Richard 190
Hitchens, Mary 191
home customs 146-153
home remedies 59-83
home soldier 49
homeste'd yarn and clothing 148
hop yeast 167
hops 69
horse 101, 106
horseshoes 39, 41
human body (superstitions) 37
hurdy-gurdy 177
Hyde Park 47

idler 170
inch worm 36
Ingomar 9, 20, 28, 180
ink, homemade 147
inkberry 147
insects 108-109
insects and snakes 108-110
Ireland xvi, 190, 191, 196
Irish moss 67

jack-o'-lantern 164
Jeely Crawley 53
jimson-weed 61, 115
Job's tears 52
Job's turkey 52
John's Island 4, 24-25, 183
Johnny juniper 115
joners, jonahs 180
Jordan 20
Jordan Bay 26
Jordan Falls 15, 147
Jordan Ferry 2
Jordan River 11

Kelly, Hugh Crosby 191
Kelly, Samuel 191
Kespoowit xiii
Kidd, Captain 4, 23-24, 25, 26
kilkid 102, 107, 152
killet 169, 174
King Street 9
knee-high buckwheat 115
knives 31
knock on wood 39, 43
knocks, three 36

INDEX

Kris Kringle 160

labrador tea 80, 153
ladybug 108
Lainrock, Betty, John, James 191
Lake Deception 10
lamps, three 38
land loom 84, 89
Lantern Views 156
launch a ship, to 179
lawery 90
lichens 120
Little Harbour 19, 127, 156, 159
Little Irishman, The 188
Little Port La Bear 4
liver pins 74
Liverpool, Eng. 182, 186
Lizzie Dies Tonight 185
lobstering 176-178, 200
Lockeport 2, 11, 14, 15, 16, 68, 84, 125, 139, 156, 159, 182, 183, 186, 187, 195, 198
lone loon 96
Louis Head Beach 15
Loyalist rose 116
Loyalists xiv
luck, bad 42
luck, good 41
Luke's dog 46
lur'd day 90, 169
Lydgate 2
Lyle, John 187

MacKenzie, John 192
mackerel sky 89
Manchester, Eng. 195
mare's tails 89
marriage 34-36, 156-157
Mary, old 8
mats 149
May Day 163
may-apple (mammy-apple) 116
McNutt's Island 196
measles 74
Megumaage xiii
menstruation 74
Micmacs xiii
milk leg 60, 64
Milky Way, Milk Maid's Path 92
Minister's green 115
mirrors 43, 44
Moger 51, 60
Monday 32
Morvan Hill 2
Morvan Road 2
Mowat Street 8, 116, 196
mullein 66, 79

Nehemiah 18
Neptune 167
New Englanders xiii, xiv
New Year's Eve 10, 160-161
New York xiv, 122, 196
Newellton 178
nippers 175

North East Harbour 66, 133
Number 13, 32

Oakpark 154
Obed, James 191
Off ox, nigh ox 103
Ohio 150; Lower Ohio 114, 115, 119, 122
onions 66, 67, 69, 72, 82
Osborne Harbour 127
Others: *Fauro* 182; *Mary Hitchens* 191; *Matchless* 184; *Ohio* 184, *Twilight* 171
ox haul 103
oxen names 103

Page, Dorcas 11
paint, homemade 147
palm branch 37
Parr, Gov. xv
Pa's cows 47-48
paste and glue 147
Pat's pig 54
patty pans 151
Peach, Benjamin 182
pennies 41, 52; pennies and two dollar bills 30
pension (bird) 99
phantom arm, leg 60-61
phantoms 18-20: bands 18-19; cars 19-20
Philips, Alexander 191
pictures 36, 44
Pierce, Josiah 182

pigs 46, 47, 103, 201
pingeons 75-76, 176
pinkies 167
pirate ghosts 25
pirates 3, 182
pissabed 64, 115
plantain 63, 68, 78
plants 114 -117: from other lands 116; lore 116-117; superstitions 117
pond loon 50
Port Clyde 25, 156, 180, 183
Port L'Hebert Rock 186
Port La Tour xiii, 4, 24, 72, 106, 190
Port La Tour Harbour 190
Port Mouton 195
Port Razair xiv, 166
Port Roseway xiv
Port Roseway Associates xv
Port Saxon 167
Portuguese xiii
potatoes 77, 79, 81
Potters Ledge 187
preachers 99
preface 133
pregnancy 33
privateers xiv, 198-199
Pubnico 198
pumpkin seeds 73

Quassia cup 61
quilts 149-150

rabbit 41

Ragged Islands xiv, 127, 128, 129, 194
rail splitter 97
Ram Island 19, 187
rambling sailor 115
raspberry leaves 75, 78, 153
rhubarb 73
rhymes, verses and tongue twisters 130-136
Robbie Hunt's barn 46
Robin Hood's barn 46
robins 88, 91
Robinson, Jack 47
rocking chair 38, 40
Rod and Gun Club 10
roosters 86
Roseway 23, 85
Roseway River 122
roundy 177
rowan 119
rules 151
Ryer, Conrad 197

Sable 19
Sable River 7, 19, 78, 81, 114, 123, 125, 127, 182
Saint-Pierre and Miquelon 181
St. Valentine's Day 162
salt horse 171
Salvages 189
sand hills 27
Sandy 6
Sandy Point 9-10, 13, 25, 26, 34, 36, 62, 71, 75, 82, 83, 105, 107, 151, 173, 182, 193, 194, 197, 199
Sandy Point lighthouse 10
Santa Clausing 159
sarsaparilla 74, 75, 80
Saturday's Moon 93
sayings 45-48
scoot horn 167
Scotch broom 76, 116
Scotch heather 116
Scotland xvi, 192
Scots-Irish xiii, xiv
scrub spruce 119
sea lore 166-202: boat and ship building 178-180; deserters 194-198; fishing 166-176; lobstering 176-178; privateers 198-199; sailors and fishermen 199-202; sea stories 180-184; shipwrecks 184-192; wracking 192-194
Seal Island 184, 191
second sight 11-12
shack cupboard 171
Shag Harbour 115, 130, 176, 197, 198
sheep marks 104
Shelburne xv, 2, 3, 5, 8, 11, 13, 14, 15, 20, 27, 72, 76, 82, 100, 105, 106, 115, 116, 118, 121, 122, 125, 126, 129, 131, 132, 136, 150, 165, 180, 195, 197

Shelburne County xiii, 84, 121, 124, 140, 166, 197
Shelburne Harbour 9, 25, 26, 182, 195, 197
Sherose Island 197
ship's knees 179
ships
  built in Shelburne County: *Billow* 19, 187; *Blue Jacket* 183; *Codseeker* 183-184; *Jennie Hammond* 183; *Nellie J. Banks* 181; *Sebim* 181; *Vernon* 182
  wrecked on coast of Shelburne County: *Amaranth* 189-190; *Bamboro* 193; *City of Washington* 186-187; *Emulous* 19; *Esme* 189; *Hungarian* 184-185; *Merman* 191; *Proud Ardent* 191; *Robust* 196; *Viance* 188; *Wildcraft* 190
shirt sleeves 45
Sierra Leone Company xv
silver bullets 20
smerry, smurry, smeary 89
soap making 146
social customs 154-156
Soeul 20
Southside Beach 183, 201
Spencer's eels 45
spiders 40
spin top 169
spinning 148
spirits, to confuse 39
spoons 31
sprew 60
Squirrel Valley 127
stars 29
sticking tommy 167
Stoddard Island 197
Stoddard, John 197
Stoddard, Nancy 197
Summerside 13
Sunday throat 46
supernatural 1-12
superstitions 29-44: black cat 200; coin beneath mast 200; colours 200; crow bad luck 199; Dennis 201; fisherman's 199-202; knives, forks, spoons 31; love's tow line 202; numbers and days 32; old sailors never die 202; pigs, hoodoo 201; pennies and two-dollar bills 30; rollers, thole pins of dogwood 202; rope clockwise 199; salt 32; shoes and clothing 32; strand of hair knit in socks 200; stars and moons 29; turn a boat clockwise 199; when not to start a fishing trip 200; whistling, knives, birds, tombstones 199-200; women on fish boat 200

INDEX

Swansburg, Cornelius 186
Sweden 191

tail an anchor 175
tamarind pit 12
tansy 64, 68, 74, 79, 83, 102, 106
Taylor 194
teaberry (ies) 114, 153
Tea Chest 25
tea leaves 11, 31
tea meetings 156
tempest 92
thole pins 169
Thorburn, Capt. Al 193
Thorburn, James 11
thoroughwort 67, 79
three generations 45
tissick 60
titters 60, 78
toenails 40
toll a bell 159
trees 118-119

umbrella 40

Vernon, Augustus 182
Villagedale 27, 111, 156
vinegar bottle, the old woman who lives in a 136-139
vinegar fizz 153

Washington 16
Water Street 9, 196
water divining 150

Watt, William 195
Watts, Ed 194
weather breeder 86
weather lore 84-93
weaving 148
Welsh settlers xvi
Welshtown 8, 122, 126, 132, 134, 142, 150, 152, 154
West Indies xiii-xiv, 16, 17, 166, 182, 183
White, Bob 47
White Peacock Feather, The 19
Williams, Capt. Colin 182
wines 153
witch birds 94
witch's tree 119
witches 20
witherod baskets 150
withewood 118
woodpecker, to die the death of a 47
Woods Harbour 127, 192,
worms 88, 91, 95
wormwood 70, 80, 81, 83
wracking 192-194
wristers 76, 175

Yarmouth 171, 187
yarrow 66

Printed in Canada